Bryan Foster

Wisdom: GOD's Hints & Tips

Bryan Foster

Wisdom:
GOD's Hints and Tips

Wisdom: GOD's Hints & Tips

Wisdom: GOD's Hints and Tips

(Author Articles)

Book 7 of the 'GOD Today' Series

Bryan Foster

Wisdom: GOD's Hints & Tips

Published in 2021
Great Developments Publishers
Gold Coast, Queensland, Australia 4217
ABN: 13133435168 USA-EIN: 98-0689457

All rights reserved. No part of this publication may be reproduced, stored in a retrieval system, transmitted in any forms or by any means, electronic, mechanical, photocopying, recording, or otherwise, without the publisher and copyright holders' prior permission. The author and publisher disclaim liability for any use, misuse, misunderstanding of any information contained herein, or for any loss, damage or injury (be it health, financial or otherwise) for any individual or group acting upon or relying on information contained or inferred from this work.

The moral rights of the author have been asserted.

Copyright © Great Developments Publishers, 2021
Creator: Foster, Bryan, 1957- author, publisher, director

 A catalogue record for this book is available from the National Library of Australia

Title: *Wisdom: GOD's Hints and Tips (Author Quotes)*

ISBN: (hardback) 9780648952046
ISBN: (paperback) 9780648952077
ISBN: (large print paperback) 9780648952053
ISBN: (e-book) 9780648952060

Notes: Includes bibliographical references and index.

Bryan Foster

'GOD Today' Series:

1GOD.world: One GOD for All, (Author Articles) (2016)

Mt Warning GOD's Revelation: Photobook Companion to '1GOD.world', (2017)

Where's GOD? Revelations Today, (Author Articles) (2018)

Where's GOD? Revelations Today Photobook Companion: GOD Signs (2nd ed) (2018) ** Author's favourite** - SO Unique and God-Given

Where's GOD? Revelations Today, Video Series, YouTube (efozz1 or CaravanAus) (2018)

Jesus and Mahomad are GOD (Author Articles) (2020)

Love is the Meaning of Life: GOD'S Love (1st ed) (Author Articles) (2021)

Wisdom: GOD's Hints and Tips (Author Articles) (2021)

Love is the Meaning of Life (2nd ed) (Author Articles) (2021/2)

Love is the Meaning of Life GOD'S Love: Photobook Companion (2022)

Wisdom: GOD's Hints & Tips

Author's Websites for *'GOD Today' Series*:

https://www.GodTodaySeries.com/
https://www.BryanFosterAuthor.com/
(20+) God Today | Facebook

+ various other social media webpages being developed.

Developing:

https://www.JesusAndMahomadAreGod.com/
https://www.LoveIsTheMeaningOfLife.com/

Images in the *'GOD Today' Series*:

Bryan Foster and Karen Foster (Great Developments Publishers) and Andrew Foster (Austographer.com)

Copyright © 2019-21 Cover photo by Bryan Foster – Amity Point sunset
Graphics: Bryan Foster and Bookpod

> Each quote in these highlighted boxes, along with the all text in this book 7 are
>
> Copyright © 2006-2021 by
>
> Great Developments Publishers

DEDICATION

This Book is dedicated to Karen, the Love of my life, my wife of 43 years. My rock, my Uluru, my heart of Australia.
And to my children Leigh-Maree, Andrew and Jacqui, daughter-in-law Shannon and grandchildren Kyan, Cruze, Felicity and Isabella.
To my parents, Frank (deceased 2018) and Mary.
And to my siblings John, Susy and Clare and all my extended family.
Thank you for all your love, support and encouragement.
To my dear friends and former educational colleagues, thank you.
What an experience and life GOD has given us. I am so grateful to GOD for the incredible assistance 'He' has given me to write this *'GOD Today' Series*, 2016-2022. If there wasn't a most loving GOD, this *Series* would be non-existent.

Wisdom: GOD's Hints & Tips

CONTENTS

'GOD Today' Series	7
Dedication	9
Contents	10
Foreword by Karen Foster	16
Preface by Author	18
Author	24
'GOD Today' Series – Overviews Books 1-9	31
Introduction	40

GOD's HINTS and TIPS

Introduction to Wisdom Quotes   49

Wisdom Quotes – a decade+ in the receiving (103 Wise Quotes)	50
Financial Suggestions Disclaimer	69
Introduction for the 21 Revelations from GOD to the Author	70
Complex Significant Revelations from GOD in this *Series*	72
21 Revelations from GOD to Bryan – 2016 and 2018	74
GOD's Absolute Wisdom and Love	77

Bryan Foster

Key MESSAGES in the *'GOD Today'* Series (2016-2021) to the Author - Revelations and Discerned Messages from GOD

Book 1 *1GOD.world: One GOD for All, (Author Articles)* (2016)   79

Book 2 *Mt Warning GOD's Revelation: Photobook Companion to '1GOD.world'*, (2017)   80

Book 3 *Where's GOD? Revelations Today, (Author Articles)* (2018)   81

Book 4 *Where's GOD? Revelations Today Photobook Companion: GOD Signs (2nd ed)* (2018)
** Author's favourite**.   83

Book 5 *Jesus and Mahomad are GOD (Author Articles)* (2020)   85

Book 6 *Love is the Meaning of Life: GOD'S Love (1st ed) (Author Articles)* 2021)   87

Wisdom Quotes in Grey Boxes - Revelations from GOD to Bryan, or Discerned by Bryan from GOD. From the *'GOD Today'* Series. Book by Book.

Book 1 *1GOD.world: One GOD for All, (Author Articles)* (2016)   90

Book 3 *Where's GOD? Revelations Today, (Author Articles)* (2018)   96

Book 5 *Jesus and Mahomad are GOD (Author Articles)* (2020)   101

     GOD and Incarnations   112
     One GOD Two Incarnations   113

Book 6 *Love is the Meaning of Life: GOD'S Love (1ˢᵗ ed) (Author Articles)* (2021)   119

Book 7 *Wisdom: GOD's Hints and Tips (Author Articles)* (2021)   132

Conclusion   137

Appendices

These appendices assist with the background of GOD's Revelations and Inspired Messages and Bryan's pronouncement of these for GOD to today's world. The following appendices are aimed at those seeking more detail or a refresher from what has come before in this *Series* since Book 1 in 2016.

Appendix 1 - Highlighted Key Points from Books One to Six - an Overview   141

Appendix 2 - What are Revelations and Inspired Messages from God?   145

Appendix 3 – Revelations and Inspired Messages from GOD to Bryan for Today's World   150

Appendix 4 - Are the Revelations and Inspired Messages contained in this *Series* the Truth from God? Genuine and authentic explanations?   154

Appendix 5 - Where it all began – Author's 25th Birthday Revelation	163
Appendix 6 - Mt Warning – Word of GOD's Revelation – the Story	169
Appendix 7 – Tears from GOD	173
Appendix 8 – Peacefulness with GOD – a Deep Personal Experience of GOD and Wisdom	178
Appendix 9 – GOD's Powerful Signs and Coincidences	180
Author's Websites	187
Index	188
Bibliography	191
Books by Author	195
End	200

Each book in this *'GOD Today' Series*

invites us in various ways to join in the discovery of GOD,

GOD's Wisdom and Revelations, Inspired Messages and Love,

as we journey towards our own personal and communal salvation with GOD on Earth, and if so blessed, later in Heaven.

Heaven is the culmination for those who have Loved GOD and others intensely over their lives

(allowing for times of weakness and the forgiveness, though)

and at the time of death

make this final decision to be with GOD forever…

We must eventually accept that this relationship with GOD is the most positive, enhancing, honest, forgiving, and absolutely loving one we could ever imagine.

The closer we get to the Absolutely Loving GOD of Wisdom, the sooner we can find out about our true soulful selves and our place in GOD's plans.

We find out that GOD's divine relationship with us all is so much more significant and impressive than for one we could ever imagine.

Foreword by Karen Foster

I have witnessed Bryan's close contact with GOD for many years. I am also blessed to have a meaningful relationship with GOD. Our primary purpose is to help as many people as possible find GOD in their lives, as we have been able to do ourselves. This latest book in the *'GOD Today' Series*, Book 7, titled *Wisdom: GOD's Hints and Tips,* 2021, shares the necessity for genuine Wisdom in today's world. It details the world's connection to the Absolutely Wise, One and Only GOD who exists forever – never beginning and never ending.

Bryan invites you to explore affirming examples of Wisdom from GOD and about GOD for today's world - for each of us in our own way. We all need GOD's Wisdom and guidance to help our lives be successful, loving, and genuinely wise earthly lives in preparation for meeting GOD in Heaven.

The seventh Book in Bryan's *'GOD Today' Series* continues discovering GOD's Wisdom and Love. This all began with Book 1 of the Series, *1GOD.world: One GOD for All* in 2016.

Each Book in this *'GOD Today' Series* (2016-2022) invites us to join in the discovery of GOD's Wisdom shown through GOD's Revelations, GOD's Inspired Messages, and GOD's Love, as we work towards our own personal and communal Salvation with GOD in Heaven. All this personal and communal development is essential in our quest for the LOVE and WISDOM from GOD.

Our relationship with GOD can be the wisest, most positive, enhancing, honest, forgiving, and loving one we could ever imagine. The closer we get to the

Bryan Foster

Absolutely Loving, Wise GOD, the more we discover our true soulful selves and our relationship with GOD and others.

In this next book, Bryan renews and continues exploring who GOD is. He *emphasises the Wise story of, and for, GOD and us together*. What is GOD's Wisdom? What is our Wisdom? And how we are to be dependent and needing GOD and each other. We can then be open to how GOD is discovered and followed in our lives and through our loving experiences.

We, the people of the world, have been given the power to develop the Wisdom that GOD has shown us, and hence that Wisdom becomes an integral aspect of our own wise, loving selves.

(Karen and Bryan have been married for 43 years this year. Both vocations were as Religious Education teachers in religious schools - Bryan for 42 years and now retired from teaching, and Karen for 39 years and still thoroughly enjoying teaching in a religious school.)

Preface

Wisdom: GOD's Hints and Tips, (2021)

GOD's Hints and Tips to the author have been developed over the past few decades since secondary school (particularly from years 10 to 12 in 1972-1974). These years contained several times he presumed that GOD called him to consider a life's vocation within the priestly clergy. This book's numerous Revelations from GOD, and Bryan's quotes as discerned from GOD, are highlighted within *Wisdom: GOD's Hints and Tips* in the *'GOD Today' Series*, published in 2021. The necessary information from GOD was sent at a vital moment within humanity's history. Challengers to GOD and GOD's supposed relevance are countered by the quotes from three sources for this book: 1. 21 Revelations to Bryan from GOD in 2016 and 2018; 2. 103 wisdom quotes, as being discerned by Bryan from GOD over a decade+; and 3. highlighted quotes taken from each book within this *Series*, which take the inspired teachings from GOD to over 200 quotes. All these messages from GOD are highlighted within this Book 7.

Who else could offer us all Tips and Hints from GOD, other than GOD! This book strongly supports the reality and unquestionable success of GOD's Wisdom for our most beautiful world and all 'His' creations - forever. The People's Wisdom is also precious for all living people, including the fauna and flora associated with our world. GOD's Wisdom to me in 2016 and 2018 was absolutely remarkable – and definitely real. It consisted of 21 Revelations, which inform this Wisdom book's backbone, and the other books in the Series, *'GOD Today' Series*.

The Wisdom of Love teaches us so much about GOD and how Wisdom affects us significantly. When open to GOD's Wisdom, we can grow so much with and through our One GOD. Our own discovered, genuine Love and Wisdom from GOD needs to work towards its impacts on our spouses and partners, families, children, parents, extended family, friends, colleagues, parishioners at church, wealthy and poor, lonely and friendly, skilled and unskilled workers, etc. In other words, Wisdom and Love are everywhere, just waiting for us to join up with GOD and GOD's Wisdom and all 'HIS' creations.

GOD teaches us so much about Love and Wisdom (see examples above). Just as GOD is LOVE, GOD is also WISDOM. Love and Wisdom are the Soul of every living organism and lifeform, flora, and fauna. GOD gives all living things a Soul and the Love we need for eternity. It is up to us to acknowledge it, believe it, ask GOD about it, plus everything else we need throughout our lives and the lives of all the people each of us comes in contact with, whether in a deep relationship way or just people 'passing in the night'.

We need GOD so much. Believe it and bring GOD on board to assist all of us in our lives. Believing or pretending to act as humans having total control is devoid of any sense and reality. Humans are so insignificant as individual humans and communities when compared to GOD. In fact, how and why would anyone try a comparison? It actually sounds so weird a thought!. But yet certain people do.

The 'secret' is quite simple. GOD became human twice, as Jesus and *Mahomad, which eventually became two religions, Christianity and Islam.

(* Mahomad was spelled this way when received from God. Both religions and GOD Incarnations were revealed as Revelation #15 in 2016.)

Christianity is very evident due to the large following worldwide of around 2.4 billion faithful. Islam is just behind, with about 1.9 billion followers. Islam and Christianity were part of the 2016 Revelations from God to me (and possibly others worldwide). There is always a possibility of more Incarnations of GOD becoming a human, but, I believe, the general population is not aware of any at this stage. Through these Incarnations, GOD exemplified and taught what true Love and Wisdom are - A LOVE and Wisdom existing for eternity for and with each of us. There were two Incarnations of GOD living life fully as humans – Jesus and *Mahomad. (Maybe there were more, but if so, it isn't yet public knowledge.)

See Book 5 in the *'GOD Today' Series*, i.e., *Jesus and Mahomad are GOD*, and Book 6 *Love is the Meaning of Life: GOD's Love*, for detailed explanations of how this #15 Revelation from GOD in 2016 eventuated and what it means for Islam, Christianity and the world today. (See Appendix 6 also)

See Book 6 also for many answers to the question, What is the meaning of life? Book 6 contains a significant exploration of this question with many discerned or revealed quotes from GOD.

This latest Book 7 answers other questions, basically on Wisdom - Our Wisdom and GOD's Wisdom. GOD's Wisdom is at the least the sum total of all Wisdom throughout history, now and into the future. GOD is sharing this with us out of absolute Love. GOD encourages us to grow so much closer to 'Him,' which is GOD and GOD's Wisdom. The closer we grow towards GOD, the greater our human Wisdom becomes and the more is shared by GOD.

I have been recording various statements I believe are from GOD, directly or otherwise - maybe Revelations, Inspired Messages, or Key Points for over a decade. It is how this Book started. It began with the 103 quotes I had recorded over a decade and more. These have been added to continually. The first 60 have been designed to align somewhat with people's ages and stages from 1-60. GOD made it clear that these are very important to GOD's mission for us on Earth.

The content of Book 7 comes from three primary sources. Each source has come from GOD, I believe, for others (unknown to me at this stage) and myself to propagate GOD's messages to humankind, in whatever way we may be able to do so. At some stage, I will need to bring other good and holy people on board to assist with the propagation. Hopefully, many of these people will see this *Series* of books, videos and websites as a means to begin to take on board GOD's Wisdom and Love in readiness for passing our information onto the world of today. I would imagine these would be everyday laypeople like ourselves, readers, and various religious Leaders of at least Christianity and Islam, but not only these. There will be a place and time for all religions to work together, now that GOD has informed us about 'His' Love and Wisdom for ALL people worldwide and forever, no matter their religion, status, community, etc.

The three Wisdom sources for this book are:

- Wisdom/Reflection quotes by the author over a decade (103) and discerned from GOD.
- The 21 Wise Revelations from GOD to the author in 2016 and 2018. Plus his 25th birthday GOD Commitment and 'Tears from GOD' in 1982.
- Wisdom quotes from inside the grey boxes in each Book from 1-7 in this *'GOD Today' Series*. Each book's quotes highlight its significance while exploring particular details and themes in each chapter.

The challenge is, what are we to do with well over two hundred quotes from the three sources just mentioned?

GOD has asked us to read and reflect upon these. Each person will most likely gain differently from each quote. GOD has invited us to be open to the 'His' Wisdom of Love and any discerned Wisdom of Love from the author and other informed people from any of these sources. Interestingly, it may be a surprise to some.

Still, the Wisdom of each may vary for the reader each time a specific quote was reflected upon over time, and life's religious and earthly circumstances abound in our search for the One True GOD.

This book requires a different approach from most books. This is because of the nature of specific quotes. Reflections by the readers should be spread out over time to gain a fuller appreciation of GOD's Wisdom and your developing Wisdom as you move towards GOD. A few appendices were added to assist the reader with specific terms, themes, and practices needed for a more complete appreciation. These were initially shared in one or more of the previous books in this *Series*.

Bryan Foster

Note:

'GOD' is spelled mostly with total capitalisation throughout this *Series*. GOD's perfection, and brilliant guidance for all living entities, fauna or flora, including humans, must be continually noticed and considered by the reader. The reader must accept GOD's divine and godly reality. The capitalisation of GOD reinforces this. It is best not to be ignored or even seen.

REVELATIONS

from GOD.

Inspired Wisdom

from GOD.

Wisdom quotes from each book in this *Series* are from GOD –

whether Revalations or Inspired Messages from GOD.

Author

There is a significant need to bring GOD back to our world of societal and smaller community's leadership decisions and growth. The secular society often makes uninformed and non-divinely influenced decisions, negatively impacting the various world populations, often in flawed ways. What do we need from GOD? How can we gain this? What does each person need to do – for GOD's Wisdom and Love?

Bryan Foster, the author, has been married to Karen Foster for forty-three years this year. He taught for 42 years and held senior leadership positions in religious schools and his Church deanery and parishes. They have three adult children and four grandchildren. Their two eldest children are teachers in Catholic schools, as is Karen, Bryan's wife, while their third daughter has graduated with a Science degree and is now doing her Honours. Bryan and Karen are very much in Love after forty-six years. There is much genuine, authentic Love. *The good news is that Wisdom grows over time. Bryan very much feels at a high point in life, even though now in his early 60's.*

The author now concentrates on his publications through Karen's and his *Great Developments Publications* company. His many books, photobooks, articles, and other writings, videos, photography and websites are his mainstay now, having retired from teaching classes from years 1 to 12 over his career. As a religion teacher in secondary/high school, he specifically taught the Board subject, Study of Religion (SOR), which counts towards the students' graduation results, to senior students in years 11 and 12 for 30 years. He was on the South Brisbane/Gold Coast SOR panel for the majority of this time.

Bryan Foster

His latest *Series* is the *'GOD Today' Series,* which began in 2016 after Bryan received 15 Revelations from GOD, one cool winter's night in May, 2016, while caravanning on the plains of Mt Warning in Murwillumbah, NSW, Australia. During these Revelations, GOD requested Bryan to begin writing the first Book of this *Series*. Mt Warning has taken on an extraordinary significance in this *Series* and the author's life. It has been in view or close by when GOD gave Bryan Revelations and many Inspired Messages and Loving support for something essential, divine or other spiritual happenings or events. The *Series* will conclude in 2022 with nine books, including photobooks, a few videos as part of the *Series*, following the discerned timeline given to the author by GOD. The latest book in this *Series* is Book 7. Bryan's writings include non-fiction books, photobooks, videos, websites, images, and social networking sites.

Along with Mt Warning, another significant geographical feature is the Sun! It was no coincidence that Bryan had received unique contact from GOD while he was at the starting point for the Mt Warning climbers who walk to its peak. Quite a number of images were taken there. The most common pics were selfies of the Sun shining through the foliage and creating what he calls sun flares and sun arrows. These sun arrows appeared to move from the sun flares coming through the vegetation across Bryan himself – the sun flare 'shooting' it out and the sun arrows appearing in front of Bryan and across his body, head, and handheld book. Books 3 and 4 detail highlights of these genuinely amazing photos. Book 4 shows these highlights as a photobook with some unique and stunning images to share with all.

Wisdom: GOD's Hints & Tips

The author has published twenty-three books since 2008 across four themes. The themes being:

'GOD Today' Series;

Marketing Religious Schools and Churches;

Videos and Websites for the 'GOD Today' Series;

Hints and Tips and where to stay and what to do and see from suggested videos for caravan/trailer beginners.

Outside of the 'GOD Today' Series, Bryan's special interests are the photobooks and videos for the beginning caravan and camping travellers Australia-wide. He shares the highlights of places to stay and things to see and do on the roads throughout Australia. There are 780+ videos on YouTube to view across the themes. These are free-to-watch videos at this stage (channel 'efozz1' or 'CaravanAus' on YouTube) and cover the above four themes through video vision.

Bryan has played a significant role in religious schools, parishes, and deanery. He has been a primary/elementary schools' principal twice and an assistant principal for religious Education in secondary/high school for ten years.

He has been a president/secretary of Catholic parishes and the deanery pastoral councils on the Gold Coast and Southern Brisbane, Australia.

The decision to feature GOD's Wisdom of Love in this Book 7 is crucial to any Love discussion. In the first four books in this *Series*, the author's fifteen initial Revelations received from GOD in 2016 have been emphasised. Along with a significant Revelation received on his birthday in 1982 during a 'Commitment Day to GOD' at the first secondary school in which Bryan was teaching. *This next Book 7 goes to the core of Love and Wisdom and GOD's exceptional loving place in our world – a more in-depth exploration of two essential May 2016 Revelations.* This is along with his six Revelations from GOD in November 2018, once again, while camping near Mt Warning. These latest Revelations highlight what Wisdom is and how the Wisdom of GOD's Love impacts every individual and community. *There is also a challenge for the reader to consider the place of GOD in all Loving relationships. After all, we were created out of GOD's Love for all people. Love must be the essential core for our development into unique and Loving people.*

People's Wisdom of LOVE is from GOD. GOD is Absolute LOVE! Everything we know about Love and its impact on us comes from GOD. Every experience each person has of the Wisdom of Love is from GOD – is of GOD with us.

GOD's Absolute Wisdom and Love encourage us to grow together as one people, one world - together with the One and Only, GOD. Love is the Meaning of Life. The Wisdom of GOD'S Love leads, guides, and supports us as we grow in GOD's Love and Wisdom and the Love of others.

Uppermost is Bryan's desire to grow as close as humanly possible to GOD and to genuinely assist as many people as he can in their quest to GOD on Earth in the first instance. Then to complete the story, as discerned from GOD, it will be each of our final decisions on what we genuinely Love fully at the time of our death – i.e., GOD or Evil. We must firstly aim to grow in Love and Wisdom on Earth. Heaven awaits those who choose the Absolute Love with GOD. *After death, our presence with GOD has already been formed quite strongly through our chosen lifestyles and beliefs while living our earthly lives.*

Wisdom: GOD's Hints & Tips

There remains that one final, absolute decision to be made by each person at their death – GOD or EVIL?!

From the Absolute Wisdom of GOD's Love that GOD gives each of us, we make this last and final decision needed to be made by each of us. We should be using our, by now, hopefully, well-developed Wisdom of Love to choose GOD. Most people will be able to do this well or at least with some genuine loving choice. However, there will almost certainly be a few whose life was evil and through which these evil people now see their only option, i.e., Evil, not GOD!

The *'GOD Today' Series,* written by Bryan Foster, is composed between 2016 and 2022. This current title is Book 7 of the 9. Its strong basis and background come from the Revelations from GOD to Bryan in 2016 and 2018 (plus the first high impact one received in 1982). Other Inspired Messages and Key/Vital Points also exist and occur with the author in different ways. These are mainly discerned from GOD through prayer, meditation, liturgies, and discussions, especially with Bryan's wife, Karen. GOD uses signs, coincidences, and other methods. For example, the coincidence in 1982 of his first substantial and genuine receival of a Revelation contained five significant events occurring on the same day and for totally different reasons. Coincidental? The Truth? The Truth!!!

- Turned 25 on that day in May, 1982
- Made his first 'Commitment Day to GOD' COMMITMENT during principal Sr Ann's healing hands praying over him. Similar to her healing prayers over many students and other teachers that Day.

- An incredible warmth travelled from the top of his head to his feet while being prayed over.
- He received his first significant 'Tears from GOD'.
- Travelled to the Queensland country to his first primary/elementary school principal position. Left that afternoon on the 'Commitment Day to GOD'.

The 'Tears from GOD' are seen as confirmation of Revelations directly to the receiver, in this case, Bryan (and many others throughout history). Plus, at other times, GOD is advising him of something essential and necessary. These Tears from GOD are different from normal crying tears, no sobbing, etc., and are used by GOD to show authentic relationships and facts with 'Him'. Historical records exist from various written sources composed by people with similar experiences in several religions. The Tears from GOD help those receiving these to feel GOD's presence guiding, strengthening, supporting, rewarding or forgiving them. *It should also encourage other people to search for GOD as best they can.*

Why the Appendices?

The appendices assist with the background of GOD's Revelations and Inspired Messages and Bryan's pronouncement of these for GOD to today's world. Even though the lengths of a few are reasonably long, the included detail is essential for many readers.

The following appendices are aimed at those seeking more detail or a refresher from what has come before in this *Series* since Book 1 in 2016. It also covers those who are reading this book as their first within the Series.

Academic Qualifications of the author:

Master of Education (Religious Education) (ACU)

Bachelor of Education (ACU)
Graduate Diploma of Religious Education (ACU)

Diploma of Religious Education (IFE)
Diploma of Teaching (McAuley College)

ACU = Australian Catholic University – Brisbane and Sydney Campuses

McAuley College was the Catholic Church's College for the training of primary teachers, until becoming renamed and reclassified as the ACU

IFE = Institute of Faith - Brisbane

Bryan Foster

'GOD Today' Series - Overviews

A series of nine books, i.e., six texts and three photobooks, along with a video series by Bryan Foster, are being released between 2016 and 2022.

Book 1. 1GOD.world: One GOD for All (Author Articles) (2016)

Book 2. Mt Warning GOD's Revelation: Photobook Companion to '1GOD.world' (2017)

Book 3. Where's GOD? Revelations Today (Author Articles) (2018)

Book 4. Where's GOD? Revelations Today Photobook Companion: GOD Signs (1st & 2nd ed. 's) (2018) ***Author's Favourite—unique, spectacular photos***

'GOD Today' Video Series (2018)

Book 5. Jesus and *Mahomad are GOD (Author Articles) (2020)

Book 6. Love is The Meaning of Life: GOD'S Love (Author Articles) (1st ed.) (2021)

Book 7. Wisdom: GOD's Hints and Tips (Author Articles) (2021)

Book 8. Love is The Meaning of Life (Author Articles) (2nd ed.) (2021) OUT late 2021

Book 9. Love is The Meaning of Life GOD's Love: Photobook Companion (2021/2) OUT 2022

(*Mahomad spelled this way by GOD in the 2016 Revelations.)

31

Wisdom: GOD's Hints & Tips

1GOD.world: One GOD for All introduced in detail the first major Revelation from GOD today and challenged the reader to search and find GOD through other people, nature, and GOD's Revelations and inspired messages. It introduced the author to the reader and shared twenty-six of his personal, spiritual, finding-GOD, 'everyday' stories, hopefully encouraging and assisting others in seeking and finding GOD. A series of inspired messages discerned by the author over his lifetime was shared. **OUT NOW**

Mt Warning GOD's Revelation: Photobook Companion to '1GOD.world' is a 72-kilometre photographic exploration around Mt Warning and up to the walking track's starting point. These were taken over three years, culminating with the Revelations from GOD on the plains at the foot of the mountain one cold winter's night. It is a photographic and written story of the spectacular and spiritually inspiring Mt Warning and its surrounding towns, landscapes, and fauna. Images are taken from most angles around its 72km base plus the road up to the walking track. **OUT NOW**

Where's GOD? Revelations Today invites the reader to continue the journey of exploring who and where GOD is for them and what are GOD's messages for today's world. It details the twelve Revelations from GOD for today introduced in the previous two books. A collection of another six inspired messages received within that same 24-hour Revelation period is shared. A key focus is on assisting the reader in their appreciation, understanding, and searches for GOD in today's world. **OUT NOW**

Bryan Foster

Where's GOD? Revelations Today Photobook Companion: GOD Signs surprises the reader with some exceptionally unique photographic images (possibly formed from various reflections and refractions of the Sun) or perhaps given directly from GOD. Some sun arrows and sun flares formed across the author, along with spectacular sunshine shapes created in the sky. Especially look in the images presented for sun-formed arrows, flares, huge Easter sun cross, rainbows, and cloud formations. These occurred at venues on the plains of, and at the foot of, Mt Warning, Cabarita and Kingscliff beaches, and Straddie, at Cylinder Beach, North Stradbroke Island, and inland at Texas on the Queensland/New South Wales border, along with Vernin in B.C., Canada. The Sun is central for many people to imagine and discerning GOD and GOD's beyond-our-reality's extraordinary powers. Other spectacular sunrise and sunset images are shared. Our Sun is the centre of our world – no sun, no lives. ** The photos are so genuinely striking and unique that Book 4 is the author's favourite Book.** These pictures say thousands of words combined. ****Author's Favourite – unique, spectacular photos****
OUT NOW

Jesus and Mahomad are GOD (Revelation #15) was released in July 2020. A massive challenge for around fifty per cent of the world's population is issued. Both Jesus and Mahomad are the incarnate One and Only GOD. Part of Revelation #15 is this Book's title. Prayer and relationships with GOD and the incarnate GOD hold critical possibilities for our future world. The first and possibly overawing Revelation that is the basis for this Book came during the Revelations from GOD to the author in May 2016. The world will be religiously challenged like possibly no other time in history. The extremists and the violent must remain faithful and peaceful, no matter their likely strong desire to do otherwise. No excuse! Our loving, most peaceful GOD allows for nothing else. GOD won't accept any violence, especially in 'His' name! One essential outcome becomes the divine example of GOD's Love – we are all equal and holy before GOD until we sin. Forgiveness from us is then required. A most profound and exemplary reality of GOD is the Incarnations of Jesus and Mahomad at different times in history. **OUT NOW**

Love is The Meaning of Life: GOD'S Love (Author Articles) (1st ed.) was released in early 2021. A significant exploration of what Love is and how it affects us all introduces this Book and is the theme followed throughout. There is a substantial discussion on the types of Love, its positive and sometimes negative impacts, and how we can grow in true Love throughout our lifetimes with our unique loved ones, family, friends, colleagues, and communities, and of course, with GOD. GOD is seen as the Absolute Lover in its perfect sense. Who loves us all equally and desires our perfect union on this Earth and ultimately with GOD in Heaven. GOD's Love and people's Love are explored in detail. **OUT NOW**

Bryan Foster

Wisdom: GOD's Hints and Tips (Author Articles)

A book of Wisdom from GOD to the author should be seen as something special by most readers. GOD is sharing some outstanding essential beliefs and lifestyle messages. So many Revelations, Inspired Messages, and Vital Loving information from GOD to today's people are shared. This book will be released in 2021. It is a unique encounter with some refreshingly insightful quotes, including some challenging ones, as well. The first group of extracts of the three collections range across each reader's lifetime and are linked as examples to that stage of the author's life. The bulk comes from the first 60 years of a person's life. How these can help each of us, no matter our age or maturity, will be the reader's challenge and genuine support as we all progress through life. People who especially enjoy spiritual and human reflections will be drawn to many of the quotes. The second group is the 21 Revelations to the author in 2016 and 2018. At the same time, the third group contains the highlighted Inspired GODly Messages found in each book within this *Series*. Each one encourages serious reflection and addition to our lexicon. The author developed most of these with GOD's perfect influence and written over 40 years. These should add or support each reader's quotes from God. Then shared with others as felt appropriate.   **OUT NOW**

Love is The Meaning of Life (Author Articles) (2nd edition) (2021). This second edition of the *Love is The Meaning of Life: God's Love (1st ed.)* book is without the considerable emphasis on GOD in this Book just given. The language and discussions will be clear and non-complex, without the often found necessity by various writers to make it so convoluted. Doing so often leads to losing the level of appreciation by the reader of the topic of Love. Yet, because GOD is the perfect Love and needed for any loving relationship, there is a limited but necessary amount of discussion on this point. The author can never minimise GOD's Truth in any edition of these books. An accurate story/explanation of what Love is and its impact on our lives is explored. People often get confused when speaking of Love, as there are several types and levels of Love. GOD is Absolute Love, and Love is what we are trying to gain continually throughout our lives! Circumstances change, and so do relationships. When we achieve this Love, we also gain God! It will be a book on Love for all people. **OUT 2021/2**

Love is The Meaning of Life GOD's Love: Photobook Companion *(2022)* will actively support the previous textbook through significant photographic images. Some beautiful and authentic reflections of our Love and our lives are the basis of this photobook. The images will sometimes be quite challenging. These will support each reader as they discover various divine and life messages and support from GOD. Combined with multiple literary genres used to enhance or support the photos, this Book will be strong encouragement for those wishing for more Love in their lives and the world. Its emphasis is on how GOD, being Absolute Love, can help the reader develop our GOD relationships. **OUT 2022**

'GOD Today' Series

by Bryan Foster, the author.

Publisher and © Copyright claimed by

Great Developments Publishers

(Gold Coast, Australia)

(2016-2021)

Available from good internet bookstores,

various libraries and bookshops.

GOD is just waiting for us to say,

'YES!'

'YES, I can!'

'Yes, I want You GOD to be the major and substantial part of my life.'

'Yes, I want to be a significant part of you, GOD's existence, too!'

'I love you GOD, and I know that GOD loves me beyond anything I could imagine.'

The 'best kept secret' is to LOVE GOD above everything else!!!

GOD is seriously waiting for us to NEED GOD and to work so as to be as close as we possibly can to GOD!

LOVE is from GOD.

GOD IS ABSOLUTE LOVE!

Everything we know about LOVE and its impact on us, comes from GOD.

Every experience we have of LOVE is from GOD – and is of GOD with us.

It is GOD's ABSOLUTE LOVE encouraging us to grow together as One People, One World –

together with the One and Only, ONE – GOD for all religions of all time!

Love is the Meaning of Life – GOD'S LOVE.

LOVE GOD!

LOVE EACH OTHER!

BRING EVERYTHING TOGETHER –

as ONE.

INTRODUCTION

Book Seven's literary style is considerably different from the previous six books. *Wisdom: GOD's Hints & Tips* contains numerous quotes from GOD that I received and discerned over many years. The highly significant years for receiving GOD's Revelations directly are 1982, 2016, 2018, and 2021. The 21 Revelations were received from GOD in 2016 and 2018. GOD told me to write these down very accurately, which I did. These GOD quote pages are following. These also include Inspired Messages and Vital/Key points from GOD to me. (I strongly believe that others worldwide would also be receiving these from GOD. They too will need to work out what to do with each?) How should the reader approach this style? There are so many notable and necessary quotes from GOD and recorded in this Book 7. How best to see and action so much essential information? Don't get lost in the quantity, but be prepared for many exceptional GODly Messages aimed at all of us. There are also those everyday points that seem so simple but are incredibly necessary for our lives today. I believe that GOD includes these because the simple ones may be essentially and critically important for us now.

Many of the *Hints and Tips* from GOD can be firstly found in the previous six books within this *'GOD Today' Series*. This Book 7 concentrates on all the quotes given to me by GOD. 103 Statements discerned from past decades; 21 Revelations from 2016 and 2018; and many notable quotes in the grey boxes found in all books from Book 1 to Book 7 are included in this next Book 7. There are so many special messages from GOD in this Book 7.

Bryan Foster

Allow yourself time to read and reflect as much as possible on each quote. After all, it is not a race but a deliberately slower time to meet GOD and GOD's teachings essential for us all today. I believe there are a few possible ways, but an initial couple of more precise methods, to achieve the best outcome from considerable and essential information from GOD. It is suggested to skim the book initially for an overall feel and placement of the style and content. Next, a full read of the book, marking various sections for follow-up later once the book is read. (Or your circumstances may require these to be explored immediately, as you follow through multiple changes of maturity and life experiences). Then I suggest that you place the book in a key place for you in your home, e.g., on your bedside table or the lounge coffee table, maybe your office table if it suits your home/work's lifestyle; next, read the appropriate pages needed by you at that time, having already read the book and now requiring serious reflections.

Reflective articles cause and challenge the readers to take their time reflecting on considerable messages from GOD. *These have been given by GOD deliberately.* You may also have various methods you like to use for this genre. For many people, this may be a new approach and read for you. There is no one and only way to approach this book. Use whatever works for you to meet GOD and reflect WITH 'HIM'. Become as close as possible to GOD from GOD's quotes through the author, transcribed for all the interested readers after receiving the 21 Revelations from GOD in May 2016 (15) and November 2018 (6).

Suppose there doesn't seem to be any syncing with your personal feelings, etc.? Best to move on and come back when

Wisdom: GOD's Hints & Tips

it is considered a better time by you. It may be a good idea to develop an 'action thought', i.e., an approach to actively link the quote to an action to become a part of your active life as you go forward and it goes with you. Of course, the process and results due to each person's age and life experiences will often be quite different. As will your chosen methods for reflection may change or develop as you explore these special quotes.

Don't worry; just experience the information from GOD in the best way you know how or have discovered after trialling different approaches. The earliest response I had to GOD was to ask GOD to do what GOD's Will was with me. 'GOD, do with me what you Will.' GOD gives us continuous Absolute Love now and after our Earthly lives have ended. So we don't need to fret about anything; just genuinely work through your chosen methods of reflection at the pace that suits you best to help you understand and appreciate the somewhat essential yet challenging quotes in Book 7. Do the GOD things, not the Evil things. However, if circumstances change, so probably will your plan, e.g., as a result of severe illness, accident or GOD's future choices for you. Always be open to GOD's relationship with you and God's requirements of and for each of us. It is always in GOD's time, not ours. Be ready.

GOD has revealed many Revelations and Inspired Messages to people worldwide. For me, it has been over the decades since 1982. In 2016 and 2018, in particular, after GOD's 21 Revelations had been given to me while I was camping on the plains of Mt Warning, NSW, Australia. GOD invited me to distribute these as best I could to my 'audiences'. These 'audiences' were somewhat limited at that stage, as I was still teaching in secondary school. Once I reached 42 years of teaching Religious subjects to Years 1-12, I retired from teaching. While teaching, I taught and led religion in religious schools in Queensland, Australia – city and country.

But I needed to do more! It then occurred to me to start writing books again but on this challenging new topic for me. At this stage in my writing career, I had already published five books on marketing schools and parishes to 2011, plus 14 photobooks resulting from travelling throughout much of Australia to assist caravan and touring beginners with hints and tips etc., until 2015. Travelling Australia is one of my most enjoyable pastimes. An Australia-wide caravan and camping magazine engaged me in writing travel articles, taking photos, and creating videos for them for almost two years. I had to stop these articles and videos when I started writing the *'GOD Today' Series*. As you can appreciate, books take quite a significant amount of time. There were also professionally published journal articles in the 1990s and 780+ free videos to help each topic above, needing propagation with others to come.

Therefore, the biggest audience I could gather at this early stage of writing the *Series* was going digital and writing books for both the ebook and print markets worldwide. I wondered how I could involve students from a different perspective while no longer teaching, having retired. Facebook pages, my key websites, and new BOOKS…became the primary option for now. Book 1, *1God.world: One God for All* began the *Series* with a massive challenge for most readers, i.e., accepting that *there is Only One GOD of all time, for everyone, and everyone's religions*. This Revelation was in the first fifteen Revelations to me in 2016. GOD has had significant input into the timing of each book's publication year. Before starting Book 1, I was amazed that GOD told me to write this major theological challenging topic as Book 1. The Tears from GOD proof was continuously provided throughout the writing in 2016.

The most extraordinary moment of change in my life occurred on my 25th birthday when Karen and I celebrated three significant events that one day in 1982 - my birthday, along with my resignation and leaving Seton College's secondary school's teaching position. My family had to move that afternoon to Tara, southern Queensland, to commence my first country principalship the following week. There was also a memorable prayerful, spiritual experience of receiving GOD directly on the secondary school's 'Commitment Day to GOD' when principal Sr Ann prayed over me. The warmth of pure love and peace was felt flow from head to toes. It was so very, very special and remains with me today.

That 25th birthday turned out to be the start of a solid lifelong relationship with GOD. One of the best results, at that particular age, from being close to GOD, is to realise that following GOD and seeking GOD's Love and Wisdom leads to many rewards, assistance, enjoyment. And, of course, being human, there will be a few disappointing times and failures, etc., over our lifetime. Mostly from our mistakes or bad choices.

The claim by so many people who state that following GOD closely can only lead to a dull, 'goody-two-shoes' existence is so far from reality that it is very disappointing to hear it continually. We must 'GIVE GOD a GO'. Be honest with ourselves and others and explore life with the beauty and Love of the One and Only GOD who exists forever. Choose to make GOD an active part of our lives. The alternative chosen by the others is to behave in a non-GOD or anti-GOD way, as if this is somehow fun, etc.

Most of us realise that not following GOD is a sin. When we choose something different from what we know GOD would like, we are sinning against the Only GOD. If sinning continues and becomes much deeper and harmful for yourself or others, you move closer to Evil. Evil is selfish and destructive to people. Rejecting GOD outright through actions and beliefs, along with many highly Evil actions or thoughts during your lifetime, leads to an isolated future after death in Hell. Their decision is shown through their actions, beliefs, choices against GOD, and ultimately the EVIL rejection of GOD outright at death.

The Wisdom from GOD was shared regularly over these forty-plus years at school and parish/deanery levels. Then, the essential 21 Revelations, which were shared and requested by GOD to be written down by me in the early hours (about 3 am) on the two separate mornings, one in each of the years 2016 and 2018, led to this *'GOD Today' Series* being created, written and published from 2016 to 2022.

I can not accept that writing seven books so far in this Series could have occurred in any other way, or at all, without GOD's guidance, massive support, and sharing 'His' Wisdom with me and my Wisdom with GOD. I now share this wisdom with all interested people, starting with this Series of books and videos and digital supports, e.g., Websites and Facebook pages. (bryanfosterauthor.com and godtodayseries.com)

What is wisdom?

'Wisdom' is the ability to make sound judgements based on what you have learned from your experience or the knowledge and understanding that gives you this ability. Wisdom also means having the quality of sound judgement. (WISDOM, Cambridge English Dictionary)

Wisdom: GOD's Hints & Tips

Without question, GOD is Absolutely Wise about everything (literally). It can be no other way for the Creator of the universe and everything about it and within it, etc. GOD created Wisdom for everyone to understand various facts and then implement multiple issues, beliefs, practices, scientific findings, etc., on this Earth, as we are its stewards.

To then be able to implement, discover, create, etc., following on from the excellent judgment given divinely by GOD to each of us. We then need to decide individually whether we wish to use GOD's judgment capabilities for our benefit in accessing GOD and GOD's teachings, commandments, and creativity. However, most of all, there are crucial choices, i.e., for or against GOD's ABSOLUTE LOVE.

This book of Wisdom has been well over a decade in the making, including the receival of the Revelations and various Wise Inspired Messages and Vital/Key points and quotes/themes. Listening for GOD's input, your spiritual reflections on the quotes, discussions with others, a considerable amount of discernment, some over many years until this final Wisdom of GOD and Wisdom of Us is found. Pray to GOD for everything you need or believe is right for you, your family, and all GOD's people worldwide.

The Wisdom quotes in this book are from three sources:
- The initial 103 quotes were over ten years in the making.
- The second source was the 21 Revelations from GOD. These came on two early mornings at each venue in May 2016 and November 2018 on the plains of Mt Warning in New South Wales, Australia.

- While the third source is a selection of quotes from the highlighted grey boxes in each book in this *Series*.

GOD is the font of all Wisdom. Genuine followers of GOD sense this font and want to become an authentic part of GOD's Wisdom and our Wisdom combined to Love all of creation as best we can. The main secret of Wisdom is to be able to share the reasonable judgment and/or action of its underlying facts about anything, with anyone and with GOD.

These quotes then form an extensive collection of Wisdom from GOD and discerned Wisdom from GOD to me (and I would seriously believe others worldwide) through GOD. Readers are invited to explore these 'pieces of Wisdom'. Each piece will assist you in your search for GOD in today's world - also, for your relationships with GOD and each other. Our Wisdom leads to people in our world requiring GOD to impact a very sceptical and divided, primarily secular world.

This *Series* especially highlights GOD's preeminent and unquestionable significance to us and for us all. There can be no question about GOD's existence throughout 'HIS' creativity of the universal eternity. There can be no question about each of us all being given life from the Absolute Loving God of the universe. GOD sees each of us as absolutely equal as people on our journey to Salvation with 'HIM' in Heaven.

These Revelations, Inspired Messages, and Key/Vital Truths are for us all from GOD. GOD very much desires out of Absolute Love for us all to believe this and to move as close to GOD as possible. Salvation in Heaven awaits all those who do what GOD requires throughout their lives on Earth.

Wisdom: GOD's Hints & Tips

Those who choose Evil ways, which are the opposite of GOD's requirements, and who can't repent due to their weaknesses and evil traits and beliefs, etc., will have one last chance at death to turn to GOD entirely. Otherwise, there will be permanent, Evil souls isolated forever in Hell.

The appendices assist with the background of GOD's Revelations and Inspired Messages and Bryan's pronouncement of these for GOD to today's world. Even though the lengths of a few are reasonably long, the included detail is essential for many readers.

The appendices aim to explain in more detail or as a refresher from what has come before in this *Series* since Book 1 in 2016. It also covers those who are reading this book as their first within the Series.

GOD is very much committed to us making the correct decisions now and at the end time of our lives to reach Salvation with 'HIM'. So many of these quotes in this Book 7 will help us live good, wholesome lives while following GOD and everything GOD demands or desires for each of us. Yes, we are human and do make mistakes. GOD considers everything. Aiming for perfection with GOD is a noble and right intention. Remember that GOD will assist you, so praying with GOD is an essential aspect of gaining Salvation in Heaven. Continue your life's journey with GOD at your side. Ask for advice and help when needed. Acknowledge GOD's total, divine place in our world and our continual need to grow as close as we can to GOD throughout our lives. Heaven awaits!!!
(WISDOM-
dictionary.cambridge.org/dictionary/english/wisdom)

Bryan Foster

INTRODUCTION TO WISDOM QUOTES

A series of authentic, discerned thoughts for loving GOD and life are initially seen through the eyes of someone of that age. The numbers 0 to 60 are people's ages and are linked with possible and probable experiences to start your exploration and reflections on the quotes. (21 Revelations from GOD to Bryan in 2016 and 2018 follow these 103 discerned words from GOD. Which are followed by highlighted excerpts from each book in this *Series*.)

(For the early years, we are assuming the thought processes… a little game. Maybe that baby/toddler, who has recently come from God at birth, thinks like this? If only we knew!?)

The first 60 years led to loving aspects that hopefully have eventuated for people of those ages. The remainder occurred for various uncatalogued ages. Each of the 103 wisdom quotes could be real for most people but in multiple ages based on their own experiences and maturity. Maybe also be different from those shown here. This is a starting point for volumes of prayers, discerned thoughts, inspired messages, and Revelations from GOD, etc. Reflections usually take time. It is suggested not to rush reading this book. Time spent with these reflections should help the reader move into each one and see how it will help them and others. Some will not, but, I believe, the great majority will have various good levels of reflection and impact on you. It did on me.

The following list is over a decade in the making - reflecting and composing. Numerous reflective occasions at various times, days, and places led to the list. A real discernment with GOD and others occurred.

WISDOM QUOTES

0 – God created the world using the Big Bang Theory. (Scientific teaching) Out of pure Love, the universe continues to evolve. With or without humanity's help!

1 – God loves purely and absolutely. God created you and everyone else as equals.

2 – Little boys will be boys, and little girls will be girls. They are not little adults or the same gender. Respect each child as you would adults.

3 – Fire is dangerous. Treat it with respect. Enjoy its beauty and warmth. Put it out before it burns the house down.

4 – Love your mum and dad. Be good. Be polite. It helps makes everyone happy, especially you.

5 – School is good. Knowledge is power. Work hard. Achieve. Enjoy your schoolmates.

Take calculated risks within reason. Necessary for growth.

(The nanny state does not help anyone, really. Fix litigation laws and allow for various risky but very possible ventures.)

6 – Be fair. Stand up for your rights with respect, and don't hurt others. Respect your teachers.

7- Change is good. Moving houses for new cultures, environments and people are unique + is a bonus.

8 – Love God. Justice rules. Don't punish children unfairly. Care for your teeth. Smile. Maybe be an altar server?

9 – Make good friends. Keep and value some of them for life.

10 – Sport rules. Develops character and vital physical skills. Boys need significant male influence. Girls need significant female impact. Winning feels good. Learn how this helps you and others.

(Laugh at the principal's jokes – you never know where this will get you.??? LOL)

11 – Develop your gifts and talents to high levels. Try heaps of sporting, artistic and cultural activities to find your unique interests.

12 – Welcome adolescence. Allow the changes to happen. Don't fight these. Enjoy your newfound self.

Don't take inappropriate selfies. These will probably 'bite' you at some stage later. Have good friends and stay close to mum and dad or carers for support. Remember, what's on the internet can always be traced.

13 – Girls and boys are people first – girls and boys second. Respect them all.

Get outdoors often. Play sports and active games.

14 – Limit the payouts. Learn to accept these for what they are. Payouts 'toughen' you up but also cause hurt. Some may get bitchy for a reason based on personal competition.

Understand why and help them, and you learn from this. Don't deliberately hurt someone, ever.

15 – Technology is good. Learn to use it properly, efficiently, and for good reasons. Playtime is good. Please don't listen to older people who may want to use you as a piece of entertainment for their inadequacies.

16 – Porn is terrible. It tries to draw you in. You will become the loser. Be careful. Violence is not a part of a relationship. Love, not violence, is essential.

17 – Sexual relationships are good for loving adult couples. Respect is better. Respect yourself and others inherently. No means NO – anything leading to rape or other sexual abuse is not on. Don't 'play games' when you mean NO! Or when you don't say No and should have.

18 – Life begins at 18 (or 21) in most western countries when adult responsibilities start. Independence is fun, but the responsibility is critical. Study hard at uni., TAFE, or in the workplace, etc. Work hard to prove yourself.

Remember, knowledge is power. It is also often linked to success, money, prestige, and self-worth.

Select a vocation more than a career. Have a passion for your choice. Vocations are deeper than careers -usually more enjoyable and rewarding.

19 – When you find your soulmate, you will know within a time frame depending on your maturity, world experiences, respectful ways, etc. Don't rush it. But don't let her/him go just because of your age, your lack of career, your financial situation, etc. You may regret it later. Spend time deciding. Discuss with friends, family and other key people in your life. Be wise.

20 – Don't rush marriage or your desired permanent relationship. It genuinely takes time to know if this person is the one for you. People can fake it for you to want them - for some time, even for a couple of years or so.

21 – Value life wholeheartedly. It can be taken from you at any time. Living is exceptional. We live on a 'knife's edge'.

22 – Live your passion - vocation/career. This should happen if you made the right study/career choices.

Enjoy going to work. Respect your boss and colleagues. Work hard. Aim to achieve and be authentically successful. Very rewarding.

23 – Hedonism lacks true humanity. Selfish, greedy people are not pleasant. Keep away from them – be aware of their influences on you and others, and act accordingly. Take care when close to these

24 – Have children, if you can, and seriously want to. And when you are ready. Indeed a most rewarding and life-changing moment. For men, you begin to appreciate others, especially your Truth. Adoption may be an option for some – it may include international possibilities due to a small number of

Wisdom: GOD's Hints & Tips

babies put up for adoption these days in western countries. (Abortion has killed the adoption option for many.)

25 – Be genuinely open to experiencing God, the universal power. Take active steps and advice for this to occur.

26 – Country towns are community-based. Get into the community. Should experience this lifestyle at some point – preferably early on.

27 – Develop leadership on a professional level. Aim for this aspect if so talented and interested. Take opportunities. Early on, be prepared to leave the comfort zone and travel to less 'dynamic' places.

28 – Family comes first. As your family grows, so does your responsibility and enjoyment within this unit. Families make society. Good families make good societies.

29 – Balance lifestyle. Needs to incorporate fairly: family, career, personal needs, and necessary commitments.

30 – At 30 - Now entirely accepted by most adults as an adult within the adult world. No more excuses!

31 – Teamwork is mighty. Life teams. Work teams. Family teams. So much more can be accomplished. A significant extension of the sporting teams, cultural and artistic groups of your youth.

32 – Travel. Overseas travel experiences enhance your appreciation of and help develop broader skills needed within the global community. Domestic travel is also magic. Be careful and aware of different cultures. Respect these.

33 – Postgraduate study opens advanced opportunities, both professionally and personally, for those interested.

34 – Network professionally. Not just for career advancement, etc., but to broaden your sphere of experience and opportunities. Legitimate and professional friendship levels are needed in most cases to depth your personal growth.

35 – Keep in touch with those you value the most. Friendships and contacts will come and go.

36 – Keep fit and healthy. Eat and drink wisely, exercise daily, allow for daily RandR, sleep well, a regular preparation pattern, bed type and pillow needed. Reflect and evaluate the day. Try not to search for solutions when off to sleep - write short notes for the next day, if required.

37 – Pray regularly. For the doubters, 'if there is a GOD' and you ignore it, there is still a GOD with whom you need to relate. If nothing else, this is an excellent form of de-stressing and re-energising. Come to GOD.

38 - Holiday. Get away from the pressures of life a few times each year, if only for a few days at a time. Don't take work with you. Don't allow work commitments to impose on you. Have at least one extended break a year if at all possible – NO EXCUSES.

39 – Take promotions if of interest. Test yourself. Achieve in higher and/or different spheres professionally, in business or trades, etc.

40 – Extra-special number 40. Now you should be genuinely feeling and believing who you really are. Purity and growth are attained through various activities related to the number 40 for multiple religions. (Principle is based on the Jesus notion of his 40 days in the desert being extraordinary – for example, aiming for purity and perfection.)

41 - Adjust your life to incorporate what may be needed but are missing or minimal, and be prepared to drop or change other areas of weakness that impede you from being the real you.

42 – 'Meaning of life' is 42 for Monty Pythonesque. Humour is essential for a healthy fulsome lifestyle, even if it is from Monty Python.

Especially be able to laugh at yourself.

43 - Invest responsibly. Be aware that the most significant risk for high gains is also the greatest risk for high losses. Learn how the stock market, investment property, superannuation, and other areas of investment work. Balance your investment risks with your financial stage of life. Seek a professional financial adviser, especially at various life transitions, e.g., marriage.

43 – Gambling is not good. Only gamble what you can afford to lose. (Quote: My Dad, Frank Foster)

44 – Forgiveness is a primary characteristic of Love. One of the most challenging necessities. Have the courage to forgive others. Don't forget to forgive yourself as well, once the wrongs have been righted.

45 – Live a wholesome, humble, and exemplary life as much as possible. Be a wonderful living example for your children.

46 – Do something special for someone every day – but don't tell them. Mix it up along with the beneficiaries. This will help someone have a better day. It will also revitalise your unique place in the universe. The butterfly effect will benefit so many others as well.

47 – Love your spouse in more mature ways as you grow. Allow your relationship to deepen continually. Be proactive.

48 - Be outstanding fathers and mothers, grandfathers and grandmothers to your children and their children. Love them fully. Be strong but fair with your children's upbringing. Be very loving with the grandchildren. Being reasonably challenging, without violence, but sincere is their parent's obligation.

49 – Be generous with the unfortunate. Time, money, and prayer are always needed. Take up at least one cause or volunteer/welfare organisation, and give what you can generously in time and money, etc.

50 – LOVE is the meaning of life. Live LOVE!

51 – God is Absolute Love. God loves absolutely. God gives us Free Will to love authentically. God gives us dominion over creation. Out of Love, we must respect all of creation, especially each one of us. All creation will have the opportunity to go to Heaven – out of GOD's Absolute Love of all creation.

52 – Key Religions' messages are simple. It is universal. Love God above all else. Love each other as God loves us. Our decisions must be based on our appreciation of God's commands, our understanding of science, and the impacts our choices will have.

53 – God does not create wars, violence, starvation, etc. Humanity does it through individual and collective decisions. If God is Absolute Love, then God gives us complete freedom. Unfortunately, so often, the haves keep and don't share with the have-nots - greed rules. The haves often have 'brilliant' but questionable explanations for their deliberate inactions or actions that harm others. No matter how hard they try to justify such behaviour – they are wrong when being greedy! As are the poor when doing likewise.

54 – Natural disasters are not punishments from God. Once again, out of Love, God created the universe and all the physics, chemical, biological and other scientific principles applied to it. From that time on, it evolved, and the created actions occurred naturally. People then had choices to make about life, lifestyle and especially safe places to live.

55 – Pain and suffering are a natural part of life. No one desires this, but we all know of its Truth. Pain and suffering often lead to better outcomes when we accept this principle. People are happy to live by the adages: 'no pain no gain', 'learn from your mistakes' or 'you become a better person through adversity', etc. Therefore, relate these suggestions and others to all understandings of pain and suffering.

56 – We can ask why? And why not? Of GOD. But the bottom line is we don't really know. God is divine; we are human. Revelations from GOD are the Truth, though, for the receivers. We can't appreciate God too profoundly, as we are on different levels. However, we can gain a glimpse of GOD and 'HIS' principles by appreciating how Jesus, Mahomad, Moses, Buddha, and Brahma lived and taught. Along with the exceptional people throughout history who have outwardly lived those principles, e.g., Mother Teresa, Gandhi, Pope Francis, and the Dali Lama.

57 – Respect all legitimate religions' peoples, beliefs, GOD and values. Base the notion of 'legitimate' on the five main authentic world religions of Christianity, Islam, Hinduism, Buddhism, and Judaism. Be careful of other various sects, cults, (and denominations?) – judge these on how they relate to the principles underlying the previous religions listed.

58 – Teachers are angels. They have one of the most, if not the most, necessary professions and yet the most difficult people's vocation/career. Their responsibilities are enormous, educating the next generation. More content and administrative requirements are expected of them virtually every year - Society passes more on to their plate yearly. Society's ills are more and more expected to be solved by teachers. Respect your teachers. Respect your children's teachers. Virtually all have your child's best interests at heart. Don't be critical of them in front of your children. Be mature if there is a challenge and approach the teacher directly. 'Pat them on the back' occasionally – remember that teachers don't see their endeavours' success most of the time, as isn't the case for many other occupations or vocations.

59 – Religious leaders, priests, pastors, and teachers, have specialist and most critical roles within our society. Respect and support them whether you believe them or not (unless illegal). You mostly don't know where they have come from with various issues, themes, etc. Their professional experiences and training are different from most other people. Their aim is a better, more loving and thriving world. A world where all people are treated justly, equally and reverently. A world where God would be seen in every person.

60 – Search for WISDOM. Wise principles come and go in a person's life depending on their circumstances, including their challenges, needs, sorrows, relationships, beliefs, values, self-worth, etc. Hold onto all the Wisdom you can. The more fulfilled the lived Wisdom each person has, the greater he/she and all of humanity will be.

61 - There is no true Wisdom without God. GOD is the font of all Wisdom.

62 - Atheists and agnostics have Wisdom from God - they just don't know or believe its source!

63. Political correctness has its place, as long as the basic principles mentioned previously are not overrun. Truth out of Love must be the central point aimed for in all knowledge.

64 - Listen to people with experience. Seek out trustworthy, highly competent advisers, mentors, information givers. Just because someone says something doesn't mean they know what they are talking about.

65 - Too often, people will say anything to get your attention/friendship/support, etc. Learn how to weed out the bad from the good. Most people are actually trying to assist you. Yet, they are sometimes uninformed or lacking experience and knowledge of what is needed. Also, be aware that evil people do exist and to keep away from them however possible. By all means, if you feel safe around likely bad people, you may try and assist them in finding GOD and goodness. Typically, only adults should do this, as children are still learning the critical parameters of Love, GOD, honour, etc. Children and adolescents - don't place yourself in harm's way!!!

66 - No more authentic advice was ever spoken than — In the physical world, if it seems too good to be true, it most often is!!!

In the divine world, GOD is the Truth. Love and keep in contact daily with GOD. Prayer is mighty. Answers may align with your request. Otherwise, GOD has chosen different results. Have faith in GOD's love of all people equally and of the assistance 'He' is to everyone.

67 - Develop your intuition so that you can initially trust most people you come across until shown or sensed otherwise. An intuitive response may be quite quick.

68 - Say gidday/hello/how are you doing/good morning/afternoon, etc., to as many people as realistically possible who you come across each day.

69 – In GOD's eyes, you are no better a person than anyone else, in its truest sense. Your experiences, qualifications, relationships, and successes may imply otherwise – yet you are not a better person. Be humble and as loving as possible within the circumstances you find yourself. Remember, all people are equal, says GOD. Even though you may make incredible decisions, these are both from you and GOD. GOD's assistance is immeasurable.

70 - The poor are not in control of their lives – who would choose poverty, lack of opportunities, no connections, the minimal experience of true Love, etc.!

71 - Many of the rich have a genuine misunderstanding of the poor because they actually believe that the poor are in control of their lives. This belief gives some of the rich a 'free hit'. It allows them to ignore the real problems and pretend that they do not need to assist those less fortunate. Wrong! Assist them however possible. It is your duty from GOD!

72 - No one got rich through spending. Invest wisely.

73 - Most people don't get wealthy through their career incomes but intelligent investments, including superannuation and other various genuine retirement funds.

74 - Start saving 10% of your income from your first job onwards. After receiving sound professional advice from financial adviser/s, place your 10% of wage or salary in places that hopefully will bring you the best result, e.g., a compound fixed interest account (when rates are mid to high), or increase your superannuation accordingly, or invest in shares. But leave it there! Mostly very difficult to do, but you'll be in an incredibly favourable financial position for the older end of life in the long run.

75 - Compound interest is one of the financial 'secrets'. You get interest on your interest, as well as on your investment. Superannuation is an excellent example of this.

76 - Be careful not to over-borrow for investments or lifestyle choices. All borrowings and their interest charges have to be repaid in time. Yours and the world's circumstances change. Don't get caught out. Investments are primarily for the long term (however, a proportion of these may be needed in times of personal crises). But only take what you genuinely need;

otherwise, the whole purpose of superannuation is lost to a significant degree. Repay whatever you take out as soon as you can.

77 - Smart investing in the stock market's shares compared to investment in property virtually equals out over time - different benefits for each. Shares are quick and easy to buy and sell. Houses take time. Some people like to see their investment, e.g., houses — this is a significant appeal for them. Seek financial advice for your particular circumstances. Keep a check on these over your lifetime and revisit your adviser regularly, e.g. yearly during good times and more often when financial trouble surrounds you.

78 - Be aware of major economic effects which happen regularly. Usually, one significant impact a year. These are often unseen and so hard to prepare for. Look for the early warning signs, e.g., commercial businesses closing, house prices stagnating or (worse) dropping, shares dropping in value, interest rates falling.

80 - House cycles. Housing values most often go through cycles — from peaks to troughs and troughs to peaks. Different cities and towns in the same country usually have differently timed cycles throughout the years.

81 - Be well prepared for investing. Seek professional advice from qualified financial advisers (and accountants for directions to initially take). Read. Listen. Converse with the experts. Usually, the more expert, the better. It pays to seek accurate and qualified professional advice. Check what their advice is based on, whether they have any financial gains due to their advice, e.g., various kickbacks and salary bonuses from such investments, which may bias their views. It is their lawful duty to explain any advantages they achieve through your investment choices. These laws seem to change relatively quite often. Keep up to date.

82 - If possible, get advice from people who have been directly involved with the investment they are purporting. Someone who has achieved financial success directly from this investment source should hopefully be of a higher value than someone just promoting their 'kickbacks' or salary.

83 - Each human seems so tiny but amazingly awesome, even though this is not so compared to GOD. But GOD does ask us to care for each other and everything within our world. (Look at the person in a rainforest standing within the enormous and multiple trees.) The power and potential to influence world-shattering ideas and creative options etc., within the brain to achieve so much are boundless. A universal paradigm is possible and expected of each individual, work towards its possibility. Yet, we are nothing compared to GOD's power, creativeness, absolute Love, etc. But God wants us to share in 'His' loving extreme.

84 – Give your full attention to the person with whom you are communicating in all of life's circumstances. It shows respect, allows for accuracy and good recall and allows each person to feel valued. Some will even become special lifelong friends, business associates, mentors, etc.

85 – Computer games, social media, the internet, texting, etc., can become addictive and diminish your quality of life. Be careful and seek help if this becomes apparent to you or your friends and colleagues. Addiction does happen, e.g., to computer games.

86 - Don't hit a person when they are down. Never stomp or kick when down - both are evil, serious actions. One punch can kill. Minimal self-defence is acceptable for your safety. Don't overdo it!

87 - Beauty is remarkable. Love it. Be responsible. A beautiful looking person needs to respect all others, just as required by all others to all people. You have a gift, most others desire. Use your attractiveness for good - be responsible, share and help others as needed. Responsibly appreciate others own beauty as a person, within themselves, and within yourself, etc.

88 - Age brings Wisdom, which is quite exciting. Youth brings energy, drive, speed, enormous hope, plans, etc. Wisdom is incredible once attained – grown into throughout life, using all of life's experiences, good and bad. Life seems so much better, encompassing, loving, even to the level of divineness achieved.

89 - When Wisdom and youth are brought together, magic happens. Young be open to the older. Older be open to the younger!

90 - Allow all people to be themselves, no matter how different to you they may be. Exemption – Evil ones. Even evil people can be saved, but it may take 'immeasurable' actions and support. Be careful not to give away your best and Love. If the evil adults don't go along with your Loving help, you may have to leave them to their own adult choices!

91 - Life truly is short and seems so the older you get. Allow each moment to be something special to you in the whole scheme of things, no matter how little or large it may be. Treat the mundane, everyday life as wholesome and the backbone/basis for all the exciting and disappointing times that inevitably come.

92 -Develop true, wholesome and good values. These will hold you in good stead. Good guys do win, mostly. Sometimes hard to see, though. Most people are good, overall.

93 - Manners are powerful. Especially 'please' and 'thank you'. Look the person in the eye, if possible.

94 - Be able to mix with the powerful and the powerless alike. Confidence in yourself and your life's triumphs and challenging lessons learned is the basis for this possibility. Mix with all sorts of people for a well-balanced appreciation of life and gain the ability to lead a life for the betterment of all people with whom you come in close contact or contact from a distance.

95 - Good value mostly keeps the economy and communities functioning well. Cheap or too expensive kills off both the economy and society eventually.

96 - Do what you feel you must do - As long as it is correct, reasonable and Godly. Asking GOD initially often helps.

97 – If male, be a man - not a wimp. Yes, it can get tricky - but look after yourself also. If married or in a loving partnership, look after your wife/partner and children thoroughly! Be sensible and don't place them in danger. Be someone for whom your wife and children can be proud.

No violence, disrespect or hate are allowed by GOD. Be truly LOVING to all, especially your family.

98 - Be open to the wonder and awe of the universe in which you are living. Don't forget the stars at night. The incredible wild and domestic animals. Our flora. Or the people who do so much for others.

99 - Know the difference between the sensual and the lustful. The sensuality of this world is awesome when seen in a beautiful and not grubby way.

100 - These are my 103 pieces of Wisdom from GOD that I believe are essential and have been formed and written over several decades. Number 100 says that I may become wiser with more experience and be open to adjusting these other 102

wisdom statements as I listen to more people, experience more of the world and people, listen to God, etc. Let's all do this together. That's WISDOM!

101 - There is never too much Wisdom if the Wisdom is the Truth.

102 – Communicating face-to-face is the most personable and trustworthy way.

103 – Digital age communication devices are a resource, not an 'appendage'. Each has its place, but not to be its only place.

N.B. Financial Disclaimer –

I, Bryan Foster, the author of these investment quotes, am not a financial adviser or accountant. These pieces of financial advice in this book need to be checked with qualified financial planners, etc., before deciding on your investment pathway.

Seek professional financial guidance from trusted sources and act accordingly. Be prepared to take action early. You may even need to accept financial losses at times so as not to have more significant losses down the track

INTRODUCTION for the -
21 REVELATIONS FROM GOD to the AUTHOR

GOD revealed to me 21 Revelations for today's people. On two separate occasions in 2016 and 2018, I was camping on Mt Warning/Wollumbin's plains in NSW, Australia. Both Revelation sets happened around 3 am; in winter 2016 and summer 2018.

Both times I awoke and felt something exceptional. Felt comfortable and free. I wondered what was going on. Then within my inner self came some extraordinary words, which I later accepted as coming from GOD. I was told to *"Write down what you are about to hear."* I quickly rushed around the caravan/trailer and found a pad and pencil.

For the next few minutes, *I wrote down everything as I 'heard it' in my heart of hearts.* At one time, I paused to wonder what was happening here? *GOD then directed me to, "Don't overthink what is happening. Just write it." And so, I did.*

The 'Tears from GOD' that I had been receiving over the years since my 25th birthday as signs of GOD's presence did not occur this first night, which was quite strange. However, when I went the following morning to the church Karen, my wife, and I were married forty-three years previously; *I received these Tears from GOD during the celebrated Eucharistic services.* It was also a First Communion Mass. *These tears confirmed the reality of the Revelations being genuinely revealed to me the previous night.*

I was then asked to pass these on to the world as best as I could. This seventh book is now a part of this process. A timeline from GOD for passing these on resulted over the years up until now. *Each time there was a year to write and publish. Tears from GOD were the main signs that all was good and to do as I was asked.*

Studying these Revelations, reflecting upon each, and discerning their meaning and purpose for today's world with GOD's assistance has led to quite an interesting few years.

The passing on of these was not just a straightforward process. While many of the Revelations seemed quite simple and basic, as these should be, you would think, some were profoundly serious and needed much contemplation and thought on how best to do it. GOD guided me through these times. The simple ones are as obviously simple to see as the difficult ones are as difficult to see.

The Complex Significant Revelations from **GOD** in this *Series* are:

1. 21 Revelations from **GOD** to the author in May 2016 and Nov. 2018 while caravan camping on the plains of Mt Warning.
2. There is ONLY ONE **GOD** for all people, all religions, all cultures, forever.
3. Jesus and Mohamad are both **GOD** – Incarnations of **GOD** (i.e., **GOD** became human at two times in history that we are now aware of...)
4. **GOD** uses signs to attract us and help us progress positively to Salvation. Various signs the author received since 2018 are – before my very eyes, the large Easter sun cross in the sky near Texas, Queensland, but on the NSW side of the border; sun flares and sun arrows going across me, at heart and brain angles, along with a published book in this Series that I handheld; all at various treed locations; sun rays in a cloud going sideways and vertical above Mt Warning; and a double rainbow above my caravan at Amity Point, Straddie, North Stradbroke Island. (See Book 4 for unique images from **GOD** – you'll be more than pleasantly surprised.)
5. All living flora and fauna, which includes humanity, have the opportunity to be with **GOD** after our deaths, as discerned by this book's author. This is a significant challenge that various religions will be asked to explain to their followers over time. See the key points following.

2016 - Book 1 – *1God.world: One GOD for All.* The One and Only Same GOD for all religions, all cultures, forever.

2018 – Book 3 – Where's GOD? Revelations Today. An introduction to the first 12 Revelations from GOD revealed to me in May 2016. Unique images follow in Book 4.

2018 - Book 4 – ***Where's GOD? Revelations Today Photobook Companion: GOD Signs.*** Unique and Original - sun arrows, sun flares, sun rays + a massive Sun Easter Cross, plus double rainbows on Straddie and moonrise on Palm Beach, GC. These are very special and often hard to believe – but are seriously TRUE. It is a significant assistance for readers to believe these images from GOD. These help with the validity for the reader about so much to do with GOD's Revelations to the world today in this *Series'* books. **Author's Favourite Book is Book 4**.

2020 - Book 5 – ***Jesus and Mahomad are GOD.*** (1) Jesus and Mahomad are both the Incarnations of the ONE and ONLY SAME GOD. Both Jesus and Mahomad are the Incarnate GOD. Also, the remaining Revelations from the 21 Revelations from GOD are revealed in this book. The last 6 Revelations were received in November 2018.

(1. Revelation #15. 2. 'Mohamad' spelt like this from GOD.)

2021 – Book 6 – ***Love is the Meaning of Life: GOD's Love.*** All alive humans, fauna and flora are soul-filled and pure at birth. Each creation has an eternal choice to make at death – Heaven or Hell (based on their lifestyle and beliefs before death and any subsequent change at death) - a Mystery from GOD. We will find this claim difficult, as it supports all living fauna and flora are soul-filled and will be allowed to go to GOD in Heaven at death.

Wisdom: GOD's Hints & Tips

21 REVELATIONS FROM GOD TO BRYAN

May 2016 and Nov. 2018

(These are the basis for the '*GOD Today' Series* 2016-2022)

Awoken and received around 3 am on both nights while caravanning/trailering on the plains of Mt Warning/Wollumbin, NSW, Australia.

1. *Be truthful*
2. *Don't be Greedy*
3. *Love life – don't take it*
4. *Respect all*
5. *Love one another as I have loved you*
6. *Die for what is right*
7. *Be educated for what is right & truthful*
8. *Education is paramount for all*
9. *We are one*
10. *One GOD only One GOD*
11. *GOD's messages to a world in need*
12. *This world is in enormous need*
13. *Cyberbullying – in all its forms, of all sorts, of all ages...*
14. *Fear rules – often from the cyber world eliminate this*

15. *** *Jesus is GOD*

Brahma[/n] is God

Yahweh is God
*** Mahomad is Allah/God*

*** Don't doubt this*

Jesus and Mahomad is God

Mahomad is Allah is God

16. *We NEED GOD*

17. *We need <u>to be vulnerable to GOD</u>*

18. *We need to continually be asking for GOD's help and assistance & support – always.*

'No big heads' – Just ask for help. Always.

19. *We are insignificant compared to GOD.*

20. *GOD is so superior – face up to it*

Believe it! Stop fighting it!

21. *Be meek & humble & real*

Detailed explanations for each Revelation can be found in -

Book 1 (Revelation #1),

Book 3 (15 Revelations #1-15) and

Book 5 (6 Revelations # 16-21)

(Spelling and grammar as presented to the author by GOD. 'Mahomad' was spelt this way.)

GOD's ABSOLUTE WISDOM & ABSOLUTE LOVE

BECOMES OUR MAJOR INFLUENCE AND GUIDANCE

WHEN WE ARE PREPARED TO SUBMIT TO GOD'S INCREDIBLE POWER, WISDOM, CREATIVITY, FORGIVENESS & ABSOLUTE LOVE

ALONG WITH ALL OTHER GODLY, HEAVENLY, LOVINGLY, DIVINE CHARACTERISTICS.

Having the courage to ask GOD for assistance throughout our lives is the opposite of what we usually think. It is not a sign of weakness on our behalf but an example of our strength.

Firstly, by admitting that GOD is superior to us in all ways and that our moving towards GOD, continually searching for GOD's Wisdom and power, carries us forward closer and closer throughout our lives to an incredible relationship with God GOD. All this is on our way to salvation, with GOD and most others of GOD's creations who made it to Heaven.

Wisdom: GOD's Hints & Tips

INTRODUCTION to the KEY POINTS from GOD to the AUTHOR

Revelations, Inspired Messages, and Key/Vital Points are from GOD to Bryan for dissemination.

This next section of quotes is taken from each book in this 'GOD Today' Series – Books one to six.

The main difference to other quote sections and other non-fiction titles worldwide is that this one contains many GOD extracts, appearing to be somewhat different, yet with some necessary repeats, from what has already been promulgated by GOD previously.

A number of these new ones is just that - NEW!

Bryan Foster

Key POINTS in the '*GOD Today*' Series (2016-2021) by the Author. (Revelation or Discernment)

Book 1 – *1God.world: One God for All* (2016)

There is ONLY ONE and the same GOD for everyone, every religion, every culture, for EVER.

Keep GOD's messages and explanations simple.

'Tears from GOD'. Not similar to ordinary tears but flow considerably when very close to GOD. Helps prove some teachings or be given support from GOD for the Truth.

Science is good! And essential for understanding GOD's creations and how we can improve our world and individual needs from GOD. Some science is wrong when it works against GOD, e.g., abortions. (One possible exception for an abortion for many people would be - unless the mother's life is threatened due to pregnancy).

ALL people are EQUAL in the eyes of GOD.

GOD's 12 Revelations to me in 2016 are listed as Appendix 1. These were received while camping in my caravan/trailer on the plains of Mt Warning, Wollumbin, NSW, Australia. The ninth Revelation is the first Book 1's central theme. "One God only – One God…."

I shared 26 stories showing how I discovered more about GOD throughout my life. The most effective and first one was on my 25th birthday when as a teacher, Sr Ann (principal) prayed over me at my first high school's Commitment Day to GOD. My first ever, Tears from GOD, flowed considerably, and a significant warmth was felt move internally from head to feet. GOD in action. I left the high school that day and moved to Tara, a small town in southern Queensland, as Tara's first primary principal from McAuley Teachers College in Brisbane. This was the Church's only teachers' college in Queensland in those days.

Book 2 – *Mt Warning GOD's Revelation: Photobook Companion to '1God.world'* (2017)

A photobook is showing images of Mt Warning from 360-degree angles. Along with the natural and human-made characteristics around the mountain, e.g., various farms, national parks, and state forests. It includes the small towns around the mountain, i.e., Uki and Tyalgum. It places the receival of the 21 Revelations in the Murwillumbah Showgrounds on the plains of Mt Warning as central to GOD's messages to the people of today worldwide.

> **Mt Warning, New South Wales, Australia.**
>
> **'Wollumbin' for the First Peoples.**
>
> **GOD comes 'through' this mountain to the author.**

Bryan Foster

Book 3 – *Where's God? Revelations Today* (2018)

What are Revelations and Inspired Messages from GOD? Are these the Truth?

GOD's 12 Revelations and 6 Inspired Messages received by Bryan

We NEED GOD and need to acknowledge this throughout our lives. No GOD – No Us!

The different signs and images from GOD. For Bryan, these included Sun arrows, rays and flares, a moonrise, clouds, and double rainbows. These built each reader's trust and belief of the Revelations, etc.

Examples of GOD's given coincidences, which help in finding GOD in our personal lives.

GOD Loves everyone Equally. Life's not fair or perceived to be that way. You can't have everything. The solution to all problems is GOD's Love. Forgiveness is essential for harmony and Love in our lives.

Every day is a GOD bonus until we go home to GOD in Heaven after our death.

The mystery of Suffering; Suffering, Us, and GOD; and how suffering impacts us all at various life stages.

Significant world changes are needed. The world needs two Reformations, one for the secular world and one for the Islamic world. The secular, western world needs critical changes to bring GOD back into our world significantly. Changes are necessary in our lives; our western world needs

GOD more involved, possibly more significant than ever. As GOD appears to be no longer required by the secular, western people, we find out sometimes from GOD, slowly but surely, why and how this is so wrong! We need GOD as close to each of us as possible. God's support, directions, teachings, etc., bring GOD's true Love for all community members to the fore.

Islam needs GODly Reformation/Renaissance-like events and challenges that the western world received hundreds of years ago. Aayan Ali, a refugee from Somalia and Saudi Arabia, who escaped both countries and became a member of the Netherland's parliament, and then a major award winner and receiver of major academic qualifications from Harvard University in the USA, in her book, *Heretic: Why Islam Needs A Reformation Now* (2015), explains clearly why Islam would benefit so much from a Reformation, particularly how this will stop the violence and bring peace once again to the regions in which they mostly live.

Bryan Foster

Book 4 – *Where's GOD? Revelations Today Photobook Companion: GOD Signs* (2018)

Author's Favourite Book.

An Extraordinary Photobook of Unique and Spectacular Images within this *Series*.

Unique and rare are many of the included photographic images formed by the Sun, rainforest and trees, clouds, a double rainbow, and a moonrise.

These physical features lead to some incredible results.

Many sun arrows are formed when taking selfies, which appear to move over the author's head or body or books he held up. Incidentally, these arrows weren't seen until uploaded later onto a laptop. Each image set forms a series of apparent moving arrows.

One exceptional and unique image is this Book's front cover - a giant 'Easter Cross' formed by the Sun - once again through a series of images. In this case, the Sun was 'growing' from a large round sun ball into the most incredible sun cross. Once again not seen until uploaded. This occurred on the NSW side of the QLD/NSW border a few kilometres south of Texas.

A physical world explanation hasn't yet been found. Photographers cannot replicate the raw images that are seen in these images. No filters used, etc. (One exception only for the appearance of the small cloud atop Mt Warning, which is the cover for Book 2. It needed some filter colouring to see the rays genuinely shooting out from the cloud. Nothing else was touched in any image in any way whatsoever.)

Other Sun arrow images were also photographed unknowingly at the various beach and country scenes. It includes one overseas image from Canada of the sun arrow when viewed from my son's backyard.

This Book concludes with a myriad of fascinating and beautiful sunrises and sunsets in Australia and Canada. I am beginning to realise how important the sun is to our mental, spiritual and physical selves. To have so many incredible, original sunrises and sunsets help us in our life balances. I am a natural sun and moon watcher who gains so much personally from these cosmic suns, moon, and cloud designs – each one highlighting the majesty of GOD and GOD's impact on each of us and 'His' world.

Author's favourite *Series'* Book.

Book 4.

Spectacular,
unique,
original images from GOD.

*** Definitely worth a good look...***

Bryan Foster

Book 5 – Jesus and Mahomad are GOD (2020)

Jesus and Mahomad were both named as GOD Incarnate in Revelation #15 from GOD in 2016 to the Book's author. This is a significant statement for these two religions. God wants each religion to work on it from their perspective, to explain its vital Truth. Revelation #15 follows:

Jesus is God [*]

Brahma[/n] is God

Yahweh is God Mahomad/Allah is God [*]

Mahomad/Allah is God [*]

Mahomad is Allah is God.

Jesus and Mahamod is God.

[*] Don't doubt this, i.e., especially those with the [*]

Could the author be a prophet? There is a question written on the bottom of page 1 of the 21 Revelations from GOD, which virtually says so, but not in an explicitly clear way. It states precisely as written, "I am a prophet Prophets are true".

Tears from God – more detail

The last five Revelations from Nov. 2018 are explained for today's world. The list of 21 Revelations is now recorded here too.

It's God's turn and time to get us all to listen to God and 'His' prophets, religious leaders, and authentic and wise holy people worldwide. The internet needs considerable attention, including devising necessary regulations and specific laws worldwide, to stop so much trash and untruths from being sprouted as correct and necessary for the new 'idealistic' world created by these keyboard warriors. They are being hidden away from the real world and refusing to 'show their faces' on most occasions. It is critical for the illegal and unethical social media bullies and false claimers of Truth to sprout their often unproven and unchallenged opinions on virtually everything. Hence, social media needs various laws, which protect people, religions, companies, beliefs, the Truth, the rights to free speech and personally chosen religions, etc.

> **Jesus and Mahomad are both the**
>
> **One and Only**
>
> **Incarnate GOD**
>
> (i.e. GOD became human, twice).
>
> Of all time – past, present, future –
> of which we are now being challenged to
> be fully aware.
>
> (Are there other Incarnations?)

(* 'Mahomad' was spelled this way by God while revealing Revelation #15 of 21.)

Bryan Foster

Book 6 – Love is the Meaning of Life: GOD's Love (2021)

What is Love? – some everyday answers

Some extraordinary teachings we must know and engage with – Forgiveness is essential for all relationships. You must also be able to correct the situation and then forgive the harmers and forgive yourself.

God is Absolute Love!!!

We NEED GOD

GOD makes our lives so much better. God speaks to us all; are we listening?

Prayer is essential for us – significant communication with GOD is necessary

GOD, Us and Love / GOD's Love / Where is God's Love?

Love's Challenges for GOD's People – social justice is our key to Love. The people who bully the Churches/religions and their followers are Evil.

Religious Love Challenges Today – includes GOD, angels, and Evil

- All humans, fauna, and flora are soul-filled and pure at birth and have an eternal choice to make at death!

God's unique, loving gifts for us. Tears from GOD when very close to God. These are different from emotional crying but help bring each other closer to God when our interests in GOD increase. Anyone GOD chooses can receive these.

- Two major Reformations are needed today – the secular world and Islam. (See Book 3, *Where's GOD? Revelations Today* for detail.)

Some suggestions for parents and teachers of children and adolescents to help their children find GOD and allow GOD to make a home in each one of them. Be passionate about GOD, creation, and people. Pray often when needed and when not required. This helps bring us closer to GOD.

The eight appendices add necessary detail as a refresher from the previous five books in this *Series*. Otherwise, these introduce the various topics covered in the earlier books in the *'GOD Today' Series* for people who have joined the series at this Book 6.

© 2016-2022 Books 1-9 in the *'GOD Today' Series* by Bryan Foster.

© 2016-2022 Highlighted Points in Book 6 as part of the *'GOD Today' Series* by Bryan Foster

© 2016-2022 Images in books that are a part of the *'GOD Today' Series* by Bryan Foster and Karen Foster. Assistance by Andrew Foster (Austographer.com).

© Copyright 2008-2022 All books, images, articles, websites, etc., written and published by Bryan W Foster, Karen M Foster, and Great Developments Publishers - composed from 2007 to 2021.

Bryan Foster

INTRODUCTION – Highlighted Grey boxed Wisdom Quotes from the *'GOD Today' Series*

One of the relatively unique additions to this *'GOD Today' Series* is the grey boxes of quotes, which appear in all but one book.

In Book 1, the quote boxes are used for each of the twenty-six personal, spiritual, experiential stories of mine taken from over the years of my life. I suggest that the reader may use this process with their families and their personal or family stories, once understood and when seen as needed.

From Book 2 onwards, the grey boxes in each book contain highlighted Revelations, Inspired Messages, or Key/Vital points from each written section/chapter just completed.

Hopefully, each box will contain a specific direction or challenge, through statements or questions, for the reader to pursue within their own time as required.

GOD originally inspired this special effect to highlight various points for various reasons. When reading these, I hope most readers will gain quite an amount from this selective, sometimes challenging, but what I find to be an always rewarding technique.

Revelations from GOD to Bryan, or Inspired Messages Discerned by Bryan from GOD.

GOD'S HINTS AND TIPS

Wisdom: GOD's Hints & Tips

Book 1

(Boxed Quotes for Book 1 are different. Each box has one of the 26 personal GOD stories or GOD experiences of mine.

1God.world: One God for all (2016)

The 10 Key Points, which have been inspired through prayer and life experiences from God and discerned over a lifetime and form the basis of this Book, are: There is 1 God Only. No 1 religion has a monopoly on God. Belief in 1 God strengthens personal religious and institutional faith & spirituality. God wants humanity to keep God's message simple - KIS for God. God loves us all equally. Be open to discovering and growing closer to God. Live God's messages with love 'Let Go and Let God'. Science is God's gift. Tears from God are the sign. (p.17 – page numbers are from the referred to book. Book 1 for this paragraph and the following quotes/paragraphs.)

God's Simple Messages – Summary. Over the many years since the 25th birthday 'Emmaus' experience, I have developed my appreciation of the simple messages I believe God wants us to live and believe. The more we know and appreciate about God and what God desires for humanity, the more we search and the more we find! These are as follows: There is one God! God is Lover. GOD is not a warrior. Love God above all else! Honour and celebrate God! Each authentic religion and denomination is an enabler of God's presence within the world. Love humanity - Each person loves life. Please do not take it. Be just. Treat all people equally. Celebrate humanity! Respect ALL. Especially care for children and the elderly. Share the world's fortunes. Do not be greedy. Care for the natural planet—the Earth. Celebrate nature! Live a healthy life.

Education for all is essential—especially education about God - justice and Truth. Evil exists. Fear needs to be eliminated to set people free, primarily through the cyber world of today. 1God.world -There is Heaven. A final existence with God. There is hell - the last existence without God. God can forgive all sins. Be forgiving of others. Seek forgiveness. Forgive Yourself. Be genuinely sorry and try to make restitution. Each person's thoughts and behaviours determine their final existence. Aim to be good. Be truthful. Be loving. Be an example for others. Search for meaning and truth throughout your life. Each aspect just mentioned, once found, share it! The body is the Temple of God. Purify the body. Do not deliberately harm it. Be your best. Try your best. Success is about your ability to help yourself and others, to be honest, thoughtful, and compassionate in all your dealings, and to make your world a more complete place for all. Materialism, consumerism, and individualism are not healthy in the truest sense. These are means to various ends. These do not put people first. We need to adjust how we operate within each of life's structures so that both God and others are genuinely enhanced and celebrated. (p.165)

Appendix 1. Key points received from God in prayer on 28/5/2016. Note, I believe that God's messages are for specific times, places, and cultures. These messages are specific for now. We should not assume that these are complete messages of God for today, but these are the messages for this moment and relevance now. Next week, month, year (?) could have other or similar messages. The following will have relevance to many now, especially those who live in similar circumstances to the western world, e.g., Australia: Inspired Messages received through this revelatory prayer moment: Be truthful. Do not be Greedy. Love life – don't take it. Respect all. Love one another as I have loved you. Be educated for what is correct & truthful. Education is paramount for all. We are One God only - One God. God's messages to a world in need. This world is in enormous need. 1God.world - Fear rules – often from the cyber world - eliminate this.

That same Saturday, but in the afternoon, I received some inspired words, which are the ones following. In hindsight, these were an actual precursor for what was to be experienced that night in the early morning. I was so excited about these that I couldn't wait to share with my wife during our nightly mobile call: God sits with permanent tears in his eyes. Not the warrior image. But loving and caring for all others. The body truly is the Temple of God. Purify it. Don't harm, poison it… illicit drugs, smoking… 1God.world (p.171f)

Appendix 2 My personal notes written immediately after the Inspired Revelatory Word was received: The following are my exact notes written immediately after receiving God's messages: I have been inspired by God tonight to write precisely as spoken to me… in my thoughts & words, as it is said it is written. I now know what it has been like throughout time. To hear the word of God & to write the word of God as it is spoken. I love God; God loves me!!! Believe – it is written. Do not doubt it is the Truth. All glory to God the Most High. Allah, Yahweh, Brahman, God. Written continuously as spoken to my mind in my mind. I have not translated, only transcribed. As the thoughts, messages came,

I wrote precisely – without doubt, without prejudice just wrote! Almighty God. God of All One true love. One true God, GOD.

No tears now??? Just write – this is the Word of God. Don't question the style or what I think I should expect to happen to me. Just do it! Just write! I honestly believe I have witnessed what was told to me & accurately transcribed it to the written word – Not to be touched or altered. This is the accurate word & message from God. Do & live it!!! Amen. Background to above. Breathing fresh air going to sleep highlighted the start to tonight's inspired writings – Feel & sense the specialness & uniqueness of instilling clean, fresh, cool air into my lungs.

It highlighted our necessity to care absolutely for our bodies & ourselves fully. Mt Warning. I have driven around Mt Warning for three days, admired it – looked for its best angles & as many angles as possible. Photographed & Videoed it intensely. Then tonight, at the 'foot' of it, in the plains overlooking it – the inspiration came. How many throughout history have climbed mountains to 'be with' or 'get closer to God'? I will never physically climb it again due to injuries, so God 'came down' to me. Met me on the plains overlooking its grandeur. Its awesomeness. It stands out for all about, just as God should stand out to each & every individual throughout the world – Equally. The following morning at Mass at St Patrick's Murwillumbah, the 'Tears from God' came after I asked GOD if what happened last night came from God and that God wanted me to pass this on… This was the sign from GOD that the Revelations passed from God to me were the Truth and from GOD. (p.173ff)

Wisdom: GOD's Hints & Tips

An aside:

Today, during June 2021. The Mt Warning/Wollumbin mountain walk has apparently closed permanently, as per news reports. Therefore, it possibly will not open again, as the appropriate authorities gave safety reasons for closure. I am unaware if people can still drive to the carpark at the mountain foot where the walkers start their journey up the mountain on a walkers' track. It has been claimed that the track has been considerably overgrown with vegetation and damaged since it's been closed due to the Covid 19 situation for about a year.

You must wonder why the track can't be cleared and repaired as needed? It is climbed by over 100 000 people a year. I wonder if this would have been the outcome if Uluru (Ayer's Rock) had not closed to non-first people last year???

From a personal, spiritual viewpoint, I have had many of my close encounters with GOD near this car park at the foot of the walking track. GOD came to me with various sun signs here and nearby on the plains of Mt Warning. The sun arrows and sun flares first appeared in my photos from here. (The time and images received here didn't occur on my photographic images until uploaded to my laptop? Now that's special!) There's only One GOD for all time.

Bryan Foster

A Must-Read:

Where's GOD? Revelations Today Photobook Companion: GOD Signs, Book 4

by Bryan Foster, 2018.

The included **images are the Truth, unique, and spectacular,**

for those searching for GOD in this

mixed-up, challenging world today.

Enjoy these!

Be open to GOD through these.

NO tricks – just raw and original.

WISDOM QUOTES in GREY BOXES from the *'GOD Today' Series* –

GOD'S HINTS AND TIPS

Book 3

Where's GOD? Revelations Today (2018)

It is a book of the Truth…To go out so far in claiming the authority to do so is a massive personal challenge. Rest assured, it hasn't been done lightly. (p.38)

…the need to accept my place in the scheme of God's plan and go and do whatever is required to propagate the Revelation or message! Each of these reasons supports the belief in either the Revelation or inspired messages being from God. (p.45)

There is an overwhelming sense of God's love and presence being intimately experienced at that moment. Words cannot describe what is happening. It is on another level beyond the physical. It isn't crying as we know it, but tears flowing uncontrollably. (p.50)

An intense, peaceful, united world based on God's principle of love is an outcome too good to be squandered on political or individual greed. (p.54)

To encourage all people, no matter their religion, culture, or nationality, they can use their enormous clout to save the weak and disadvantaged within their societies and the world. (p.54)

I then started to get a message to write down what I was about to receive. I soon realised that, just as in ancient times, the mountain was a conduit to God. (p.60)

We need God's help to fully and comprehensively be free of greed. Why? Because to not be greedy makes you anticultural or at least quite different from most people. Fighting the culture of the nation is extremely difficult on its own. (p.67)

All people could be fed adequately if we all so desired – even if just the wealthy and powerful desired this and then implemented it. All people could have a reasonably balanced existence with food, clothing, adequate health options, shelter, security, career options, and all those freedoms most 'would die for' and many do in trying. (p.68)

We must acknowledge the Godness (goodness) in every human. (p.72)

It is an incredibly awesome unselfish move, away from the human ego and towards the absolutely loving invitation from God. The person accepts God's invitation and becomes as close to God as humanly possible. The person takes on God's loving characteristics and lifestyle, as exemplified through Jesus and God's prophets, holy people, and outstandingly good Godly people. (p.76)

What is truthful is all that comes from God. It is through God that we come to know the Truth. It is with God's help that we live the Truth. (p.78)

The power we need comes from God and is the power of love. It is the power to assist all people. (p.80)

Wisdom: GOD's Hints & Tips

A lifetime's journey will come down to that last, most intimate of intimate moments with our One and Only Creator. That's ABSOLUTE LOVE!!! (p.83)

Believing in One God is very freeing. It has made my appreciation of my religion and all it stands for and teaches so much more profound. (p.91)

Once again, it is worth noting how so much from each religion points to one God only. (p.98)

The threat against a more equitable world lies within its economic and political systems, within the basic greed inherent within the 'haves' of humanity. The fear of the unknown in those communities being challenged to share more. And a western world day after day loses an appreciation of God's place within their lives and their world. (p.106)

I have been inspired by God tonight to write precisely as spoken to me…in my thoughts & words, as it is said it is written. (p.112)

Your Soul is the spirit of God for you. Your oneness with God. Your Soul is in your Temple of God. (p.124)

'Do no harm.' A medical person's mantra. It must also be ours as well. (p.129)

There was this incredible feeling of heat flow from my head downwards to my feet. I then broke down and cried tears of absolute love for God and those around me. This is the moment in time that all my confusion, doubts, and challenges about God disappeared. (p.135)

The closer I get to God, the more significant the impact of the sun. The sun seems to be so often at the centre of my spiritual and religious development with God. So much so that God now gives regular support through messages from the sun as these appear photographically. (p.152)

What made these appear is the divine question? God often works through nature and people. (p.158)

Once we can forgive and be forgiven, we are set free. We can live more peaceful, fulfilling lives (p.180)

You haven't truly lived until you know you are truly alive! (p.187)

The truly most powerful, most LOVING reality of God invites us home! The most comforting and loving moment of our whole lives happens in that instant! We are embraced, brought in, and become one, once again just as before we were born, with GOD! Our lives are now complete. (p.190)

We become one with God. We are now an integral part of God's absolute love. We are love! (p.192)

Science is a gift from God. Ultimately, science helps us discover God. We see God in all the intricacies and uniqueness of creation, natural and human-made. We marvel at the awe of it all. (p.198)

Science must be constructive and loving. It needs to enhance humanity, to make personhood so much more authentic. If decisions are not made from love and respect and for all the right reasons, it cannot be good. (p.200)

The world needs two new Reformations. Both the Western and Islamic worlds urgently need reform. The western world

Wisdom: GOD's Hints & Tips

needs to be more religious; the Islamic world needs to enter the 'new' world. A better balance is required. (p.210)

[*Ayaan Hirst Ali, a former Muslim from Somalia and later Saudi Arabia] challenges all Muslims to debate and challenge all those involved with this violence within Islam. And to then clearly and absolutely reject all violence. (p.217)

God always finds a way. God's Revelations and Inspired Messages are for all people, all of us equally – believers and non-believers alike. (p.229)

If I wasn't of this belief, I shouldn't, and most likely couldn't, have written the books. These Revelations and inspired messages are mostly not personal views but are from God. (p.245)

Additional points for clarity -

GOD has revealed most views for me to transcribe each into the written Word to be able to propagate each fact from GOD in whatever way suits GOD. And to the most prominent groups possible so that as many people as possible can receive GOD's Word.

Ayaan is the author of a most powerful book that strongly seems for the reader to have been written to challenge the world to convince Muslims, particularly ISIS and Al-Qaeda, to stop the killings in the name of GOD. Violence should always be a last resort. GOD doesn't support their idea of violence, except when life is legitimately threatened with death.

*Ayaan Hirsi Ali, *Heretic: Why Islam Needs a Reformation Now*, 2015, Harper Collins, New York.

Bryan Foster

WISDOM QUOTES in GREY BOXES from the *'GOD Today' Series* –

GOD'S HINTS AND TIPS

Book 5

Jesus and Mahomad are GOD (2020)

1. Incarnation Revelations of #15 - 'Jesus and Mahomad are GOD' (See p.58ff p118ff) 2. Revelation #6 - This Revelation will challenge many people as to their commitment to God and God's communities in particular. 'Die for what is right'. (See p155ff). 3. The author as a Prophet Statement (See p20ff, 135ff) 4. God's photographic sun signs help inspire us to believe in God and His loving ways for each of us. God is challenging us to accept the Revelations and inspired messages from 'Him' through his prophets and good, holy people. Often, from the ordinary come the extraordinary, Godly Revelations and challenges. (See Book 4, a photobook, and GodTodaySeries.com website.) (p.29)

The faithful, especially those from Christianity and Islam, need to find the Truth of these Revelations for their followers and other community members. The critical focus of Revelation #15 is on Islam and Christianity. Yet, it could also apply to other religions showing particular interest in God's Incarnation, etc. Book Five also brings together God's key points and teachings to the author and developed in this *Series* as clear and concise Revelations and inspired messages from God. (p.33)

(NB. 'Mahomad' was mainly spelled this way in Revelation #15 when given to the author by GOD in 2016.)

Prayer and our relationships with the Incarnate God - Jesus and Mahomad - hold essential critical possibilities for this world's future. And its people. Seek from God an informed understanding. We must ACT NOW!!! (p.49)

Referencing Note The reader will notice a general minimalisation of academic references. Where helpful, these are included. However, most of the book's content is either directly from God as Revelations or Inspired Messages discerned by the author, making considerable use of the primary source of all primary sources available - GOD. There are referrals back to Books One to Four and various appendices from the *'GOD Today' Series*. It is a necessity of background knowledge needed to help the reader understand and appreciate what God has done for Today's people worldwide. These incorporate all genuine religions; in whatever depth, they decide to be involved. (p.56)

God is telling the world that the right time is now!!! It is GOD'S Time NOW! God requests us to Reflect on Revelation #15 in-depth. (p.57)

Revelation #15 from God to the author in May 2016. Jesus is God [*] Brahma[/n] is God Yahweh is God Mahomad/Allah is God [*] Mahommad is Allah is God. Jesus and Mahamod is God. [*] Don't doubt this (*) Asterix stands for the joining of these two Revelations (with lines on the written Revelations initially) i.e., to join lines beginning with 'Jesus' and 'Mahomad'. Plus, the instruction to not doubt these two lines' authenticity. Spelling and punctuation are exactly as written from the Revelation. (p.58)

Jesus is GOD! Mahomad* is GOD! There is only 1 God for * all religions * all people * all cultures * for all time, FOREVER!!! (p.59)

Both Christian and Muslim religious leaders, theologians and scriptural scholars, etc., need to explain what Revelation #15 means for today's world, how it is possible, and how it is the Truth from God. There must also be room for other genuine religions to come to the table too, particularly Hindus and Jews who also both believe in One God. (p.60)

These two incredible Incarnate GOD Revelations where God becomes fully human are explained. The Truth of these as part of the 21 Revelations received in May 2016 and November 2018 will be clarified. The author's role in the receival of these 21 Revelations and the dissemination will be explained. Why and how is the author a part of this promulgation? How can everyone gain as a result of these? (p.60)

Islam's Mahomad is God, Christianity's Jesus Christ is God. God became Incarnate, once as Jesus around 3BCE and the next time as Mahomad around 570CE. (p.63)

"I am a prophet Prophets are true." This statement has remained there on the first of two pages of the Revelations from God received in 2016 for almost four years until recently without the author realising the implications and possible realities. The impact on me has been overwhelmingly palpable, beautiful, and inspirational. Time will tell how this will eventuate. An incredible challenge for the author. (p.69)

As the world becomes more educated and individualistic, people, communities, and societies worldwide also become more critical of much that is institutional. This criticism is particularly of institutions with considerable history. Religion is one of, if not the oldest of most cultures' institutions. It is often the first to be attacked from so many fronts. (p.73)

...the need to accept my place in the scheme of God's plan and go and do whatever I required to propagate the Revelation or message!... Each of these ten reasons (p.75ff) supports the belief in the Revelations and inspired messages being from God. As do the following explanations in this article. (p.81)

There is an overwhelming sense of God's love and presence being intimately experienced at that moment. Words cannot describe what is happening. It is on another level beyond the physical. It is not crying or sobbing as we know it, but tears incredibly, lovingly, flowing uncontrollably -Tears from God. (p82ff)

*And then the question of all questions from the depths of my whole being - **"Are you prepared to be a prophet for me [God]?" Tears from God immediately followed this question.** Indeed, it was a request from God as per such criteria noted in a few of this Series' books. It was not forced, not coerced. Just a quiet yet strongly felt request! Karen (my wife) witnessed these Tears from God events as it occurred. (p.92)*

God has strongly guided this Series' publication's content and processes. It seems genuine when I was aware of it being offered through the written Word and Tears from God. Karen witnessed the Tears. So basically, I don't know the answer yet??? I do know that God wants me to write and communicate. I also seem to feel a strong calling to be a part of this honoured role for God. As far as I can tell, God has asked me to be a prophet through the written Word and

Divine thoughts. I have received Revelations, Inspired Messages, and religious discernment from God over the decades, especially these recent five years. So Is being a prophet true? (p.97)

Expert combined groups of theologians, scriptural scholars, and others from Christianity, Islam, Judaism, and Hinduism, possibly along with other authentic religions, need to pray, consult, study, reflect, research, and discern these latest Revelations from God. And explain to all humanity in non-complicated languages how these may help a troubled world. (p.101)

People worldwide are now challenged to accept that Only One God exists for all people, religions, and cultures -forever. (p.106)

God's revealing of these at this time in history shows that humanity is now ready to receive the latest and most complete Revelation of all. (p.109)

It is now up to the religious scholars, theologians, and leaders of all interested religions, especially Christianity and Islam, to analyse these Revelations and accept these as Truth from God. To promulgate and explain these for a divided world to move towards oneness with God and each other! (p.111)

IT'S TIME!!! WE MUST DO IT!!! (p.113)

It's time for people to stop believing that only they or their religion/group have the answers, whether religious or secular. The world is at the most challenging crossroads. (p.113)

It is now the era for all authentic religions to finally come together and discover how most of these claims can be so for everyone and every religion. (P.113)

Wisdom: GOD's Hints & Tips

Science and technology are God's gifts to help us understand God and creation and for humanity to then use this knowledge to make the world a better place for everyone. (p.117)

Any violence resulting from this Revelation by any people will be seen by God/Allah as EVIL, with the appropriate response eventually forthcoming from God. No religion will honestly need to encourage the evil of violence after reading and analysing this Revelation. It is a beautiful Revelation for all! Its impact should be extra-special for all. (p.120)

All our false claims of human superiority, magnificence, and ability to do anything we want are over. We can't do everything on our own. We are mere mortals living on a knife-edge....have we medically extended life's timeline well beyond what is best for us?!...We belong to God forever and therefore are strongly invited to believe, act and do as God instructs. (p.124)

It will all happen when God so chooses. (p.126)

God makes everything very clear to anyone who wants to know. God is not out there to trick us. Absolute Love for us doesn't allow for 'tricks'. We belong to God forever and therefore are strongly invited to believe, act and do as God instructs. Actively and honestly, search for God in our lives. (p.126)

GOD said to face reality! God says it is time. God is here to guide us through the process. *All God needs is – us to genuinely say yes by our thoughts and actions!!!* Then be very open to what comes next from God. Time isn't relevant. (p.127)

God Calls Us All to Follow 'Him'. (p.131)

Hence, it will be ideal if all genuine religions could engage with this crucial modern Revelation #15 – after all, it is from God for humanity. (p.132)

Never before have our religious leaders and their advisers, scholars, theologians, etc., been required to explain why this Revelation #15 is correct - as it is a new God Revelation from our era - 2016. They also need to explain the significant ramifications of these two religions [Christianity and Islam]. There is also considerable room for other faiths to join in. Advised God (p.133)

God's Revelations # 1-21 - Be Truthful Don't be Greedy Love life – don't take it Respect all Love one another as I have loved you Die for what is right Be educated for what is proper & truthful Education is paramount for all We are one - One God only One God ("I am a prophet Prophets are true"??? This is the physical placement by number along with its punctuation in the Revelations received, i.e., after number ten and on the right lower side of the page.) God's messages to a world in need This world is in an enormous condition of being Cyberbullied – in all its forms, of all sorts, of all ages. Fear rules – often from the cyber world eliminate this God is Jesus & Mahomad* We need God We need <u>to be vulnerable to God</u> We need to continually ask for God's help and assistance & support – always. 'No big heads' – Just ask for help. Always. We are insignificant compared to God God is so superior – face up to it. Believe it! Stop fighting Be meek & humble & real (Revelations to the author in 2016 and 2018. Received at the base of Mt Warning, NSW, Australia. Written here exactly as received from God.) (p.135f)

Wisdom: GOD's Hints & Tips

We need God! God needs us - Out of love! (p.139)

Once we accept the need for God and start developing our relationship with God, we progress towards God. We can initially become one with God while still living our lives on this earth. (p.139)

This is how we must react and respond to our GOD! We must accept who we are and where we are on this divine continuum. (p.141)

We must show absolute vulnerability to our most loving GOD. That is our love for GOD! A love where we don't question, put on trial, challenge or judge! (p.141)

We must accept that we are dependent on God for everything! Yes, we have Free Will and an informed conscience to decide, yet God is there for us on every occasion we have – for every day, hour, minute, and second of our existence. We live on a knife's edge, where anything could go wrong or right at any time! We need God to guide and direct us accordingly....We have to respond as God requires! (p.144)

God desires for all of us to be saved. To meet God 'face-to-face' in Heaven. God's love for each individual is so far beyond what we can imagine that we must allow this relationship to grow, prosper, and become our everyday reality. (p.146) We need God well beyond whatever we had imagined! We can admit our station in life and legitimately turn to God for that essential support we need as humanity. (p.147)

When we accept that God is on our side and wants the best for all of us, many outstanding results will occur. (p.147)

A significant redirection back to God is called for by God! (p.150) There is no doubt at all that 'God is real & ultimately superior', that humankind must face up to it. Believe it! (p.150)

Too many people individually or communally are drifting along figuratively, some in the gentle wash of slow-moving water, others being caught in a tornado and thrown every which way.

God demands much better than this. It all comes back to LOVE, LOVE GO + LOVE EVERYONE (P.152)

Being meek, humble, and authentic is a significant challenge for many. Yet, this is what God has revealed for us to be like. Only genuine, faithful, solid, and holy people can 'be meek & humble & real' in its truest religious sense. (P.153)

Revelation 6. Die for what is right. Revelation 13. Cyberbullying – in all its forms, of all sorts, of all ages. Revelation 14. Fear rules – often from the cyberworld – eliminate this. Revelation #15. Jesus and Mahomad is God ('is' on the last line above is the actual word received and written as told by God – how can this be interpreted or explained? Both Jesus and Mahomad are the same God. The question is, why would God do this? (Is it a code for something? Does someone else know the code and is waiting for its arrival? Etc. Very strange!) (P.154)

It must be remembered that even though life is absolutely sacred and extraordinary, and that it is our human duty to value it uppermost and save it wherever and whenever possible, there may be times when we have to offer the ultimate sacrifice and die for what is right, possibly on a significant societal scale. (P.160)

Reader: What would it take for me to place my life on the line to save others or myself? Could I do it if the urgency arose? (P.160)

When the loud radical minority has the cyber ability and other media outlets to shut down genuine debate and different opinions, we are in serious trouble as a world of various differing and valuable cultures and religions. (P.163)

The more we become aware of the sustained and significant influence of the cybersphere's fearful impact on each of us, the more powerful our need is to address these influences just to remain safe, thoughtfully, and in control of our lives. (p.167)

The historical juncture to which we are now placed has the two largest religions, Christianity and Islam, being told that one of their significant beliefs is shared across both these religions. That God became Incarnate in both faiths, i.e., God became human at two specific times in history, we are now aware of the first (Jesus) and sixth/seventh (Mahomad) centuries. God lived totally as a human, as Jesus Christ and Mahomad, amongst 'His' earthly creation and eventually went back as God in Heaven. (p.173)

I then started to get a message to write down what I was about to receive. I soon realised that, just as in ancient times, the mountain was a conduit to God. (p181)

I am now an author and publisher of non-fiction books, videos, and photographs. (p.190) There was this incredible feeling of heat flow from my head downwards to my feet. I then broke down and cried Tears from God - of absolute love for God and those around me. This is the moment in time that all my confusion, doubts, and challenges about God disappeared. (p.195)

The violent Islamic fundamentalists, e.g., ISIS and Al-Qaeda, and all others who profess violence from any faith, along with individual secular groups and deniers of God, must STOP NOW!!! God demands!!! The world desperately needs true, genuine, authentic LOVE. The ONLY source of such Love is GOD! Keep in regular contact with God! Continually develop your Wisdom of Love. Work to become much closer to, and with, GOD through the – Wisdom of GOD's Love.

> The world desperately needs true, genuine, authentic LOVE.
>
> The ONLY source of such Love is GOD!
>
> Keep in regular contact with God!
>
> Continually develop your Wisdom of Love.
>
> Work to become much closer to, and with,
>
> GOD through the
>
> Wisdom of GOD's Love.

GOD and INCARNATIONS

One GOD ONLY! (For all religions, forever)

The last two Revelations in this collection of Revelations received by the author follow two themes. The first is in line with the original theme of this *'GOD Today' Series* - an emphasis is on there being only One God for all religions for all time, forever.

These final Revelations are significant yet follow the previously listed themes and discussed 15 Revelations received by the author in May 2016. The first 15 were all listed in the first four books of the series and explained in detail in the third book.

These last Revelations emphasise the earlier 'One God only – One God' Revelation and link the significant two world religions of Christianity and Islam. The One God, Only Incarnate, is explicitly listed as Jesus and Mahomad.

"Jesus is God. Brahma/n is God. Yahweh is God. Mahomad is God."

Many people would have little difficulty accepting that this 'GOD' is, or at least could be, the One and Only God of all time. The author's firm belief is that God has spoken specific Revelations to him, stating this explicitly, i.e., 'One God only – One God'. Reasons for this belief are detailed in Book 1.

People worldwide are now challenged to accept that there is only one God for all people, religions, and cultures forever. (p.105ff)

Bryan Foster

One GOD - Two Incarnations of GOD

The second theme of these last two Revelations from the 2016 Revelations from GOD is the most challenging and most likely very difficult for most people to accept. Yet this Revelation was explicitly stated by God during the Revelations to the author in 2016. Not only explicitly stated but with the added directive from God to 'Don't doubt this.' Having said this, it is still quite challenging for the author at this stage to publish it.

The author's challenge is that it is entirely against everything he has been taught as a Christian and a world religion teacher. Neither of the two religions concerned, Islam and Christianity, has ever, to his understanding, made these claims. Yet, these need to be made at the appropriate time as dictated by God.

As previously explained in the third book, it has become obvious to the author that even though God revealed the first fifteen Revelations in one go in 2016, there is an actual timeline on which God requires various Revelations to be published. At this stage, the first two books emphasised that there is 'One God only – One God'. In contrast, all the first twelve of fifteen Revelations were detailed in Book 3. Book 4 was a necessary companion to Book three, especially on the author's relationship with God.

The final theme is an Incarnation theme, i.e., God becoming fully human.

For over two thousand years, Christians have claimed that Jesus the Christ is the Incarnation of God. As a Christian, I fully believe this intrinsically. However, no other religion accepts this belief fully. The best some other religions do is accept Jesus as a prophet, e.g., Islam and Judaism. Similar to Christians, he maybe became an enlightened one in Hinduism and merged with the Godhead at his death.

Yet with these most recent Revelations from God, God goes that next step.

God's revealing of these at this time in history shows that humanity is now ready to receive the latest and most complete Revelation of all.

Mahomad is Allah i.e. God. Jesus and Mahomad are God.

Jesus and Mahomad are very similar. They are both Incarnate God. God became a fully complete human in the form of Jesus and Mahomad. So around 500 years after Jesus returned to be God in Heaven, He returned to be Mahomad for the Muslims.

How on Earth could this be possible?

The essential response is quite simple, why couldn't it be so? The One and Only God of the universe of all time and for all creation - can do anything!

But what of the previous teachings and patterns of doctrine and beliefs over millennia? How can these change? These haven't changed; each has developed. Once the perspective of there being only one God for all people and religions for all time is accepted, the apparent 'block' or reticence to compare various religions' beliefs and practices needs to be eliminated. In the first instance, Christians, Muslims, and Hindus need to work very closely together to gain a fuller, more complete appreciation of these incarnations of the one God.

There will be those who argue that, at times, the ethics of both Jesus and Mahomad are quite different, particularly regarding the place of violence. There will be those who strongly argue that it is anathema to make such Incarnate claims about Mahomad. Their particular view of God, i.e. Allah is God and Mahomad is not, is the only correct one. But this is now incorrect. Islam needs to bring this to reality in today's world.

It is now the era for all religions to finally come together and discover how these claims can be so.

The 'why' as to how can these be so, I believe, has already been answered – there is Only One GOD!

God is calling on all people to engage with one another to bring humankind together.

Of course, it will not be easy! Of course, it will be a significant change for many, if not most – but it is time!!!

People have to stop the fighting. Stop the claims of salvation being only for their few religious followers.

In the cyber-global world of today, everything is possible. We now have the technology to make it happen. We can certainly bring people together far more successfully than ever before.

The only thing which will hold us up will be the prejudices, mistrust and even hate various people, societies, and religions espouse or believe. IT'S TIME!!! WE MUST DO IT!!!

It's time for people to stop believing that only they have the answers, whether secular or religious. The world is at a crossroads.

Science and technology are God's gifts to understand God and creation and use it to make the world a better place for everyone.

Don't think that today's technology was some hit-and-miss experience of some fortunate scientists. There is undoubtedly an aspect of this in any scientific discovery, yet we need to accept the guidance God has given these people along the way. We, as humans, are not alone. *We are guided by a supreme force – the creator of the universe.* Can anyone honestly actually believe that the universe and everything in it is an accident? Fell into existence on its own? NO WAY!

World, it is time to face reality!!!

All our false claims of human superiority, magnificence, and ability to do anything we want are over. We can't do everything on our own. We are mere mortals living on a knife-edge. Can anyone honestly say they have the power to extend their lives even for one more minute if that is not God's Will? No. We might improve our life's quality and hence our potential for more life, but if our timing is different from God's, ultimately, it won't happen. For example, most people know of the very fit and healthy individuals of most ages who die from illness, injury, or self-infliction.

Life and death are so complex and complicated that except for some minor ability to extend life or its quality as humans, we have a minimal say in our lifespan.

Therefore, an excellent reason to make this happen is also quite simple – **GOD SAID TO!!!**

Bryan Foster

God says it is time.

God is here to guide us through the process.

All God needs is – US TO SAY YES!!!

<u>Revelations #15 Received May 2016:</u>

> Jesus is God [*]
>
> Brahma/[n] is God
>
> Yahweh is God
>
> Mahomad/Allah is God [*]
>
> [*] Don't doubt this
>
> Mahommad is Allah is God
>
> Jesus and Mahomad is God

[Author adds (*) Asterix to show line links on original Revelation from GOD.]

On this page are the exact words, except the punctuation [*]. (*) The Asterix shows the link between the first and fourth lines and from this join line to the fifth line. The direction was not to doubt the joined lines 1 and 4.

The line, 'Mahomad is Allah is GOD', was written on the right side of the #15 table, i.e., to where it is now.

Wisdom: GOD's Hints & Tips

N.B.

'Mahomad' was predominantly spelled this way by God in the 2016, Revelations. Plus once as 'Mahommad'. Due to this, the author maintained GOD's majority spelling throughout the book and the *Series*.

Revelations 16 to 21 were revealed to the author in 2018 after Book 3 was published. These Incarnate claims then become part of the revealed Revelations through books 4 and 5.

Text and images © Copyright 2016-21 Bryan W Foster for Great Developments Publishers. The 'GOD and Incarnation's section' was written in Vernon, BC, Canada, on Oct 1-2, 2018.

(p.107ff)

Bryan Foster

WISDOM QUOTES in GREY BOXES from the *'GOD Today' Series* –

GOD'S HINTS AND TIPS

Book 6

Love is the Meaning of Life: GOD's Love (2021)

Each book in this *'GOD Today' Series* invites us in various ways to join in the discovery of GOD, GOD's Revelations, Inspired Messages, and Love, as we journey towards our own personal and communal salvation with GOD on Earth and later in Heaven. (p.18)

We can accept that this relationship with GOD is the most positive, enhancing, honest, forgiving, and absolutely loving one we could ever imagine. The closer we get to the Absolutely Loving GOD, the closer we can find out about our true soulful selves. We find out that GOD's divine relationship with us all is so much more significant and impressive than for one we could forever imagine. (p.18)

GOD is just waiting for us to say, 'YES!' 'YES, I can!' 'Yes, I want You, GOD, to be a major and substantial part of my life.' 'Yes, I want to be a significant part of you, GOD's existence, too!' 'I love GOD, and GOD loves me beyond anything I could imagine.' The 'best-kept secret' is to LOVE GOD above everything else!!! GOD is seriously waiting for us to NEED GOD and work to be as close as we possibly can to GOD! (p.30)

LOVE is from GOD. GOD IS ABSOLUTE LOVE! Everything we know about LOVE and its impact on us comes from GOD. Every experience we have of LOVE is from GOD – and is of GOD with us. GOD's ABSOLUTE LOVE encourages us to grow together as One People, One World – together with the One and Only, ONE – GOD for all religions! *Love is the Meaning of Life – GOD'S LOVE.* LOVE GOD! LOVE EACH OTHER! BRING EVERYTHING TOGETHER – as ONE. (p.34)

GOD is always correct. GOD's instructions to us are always the Truth. Everything we genuinely feel right and positively about and with GOD is most likely the Truth. However, be careful not to misinterpret everything being from GOD. Discerning the Truth is so necessary. GOD and GOD's awesome goodness is humanity's primary aim and intention for life! (p.47)

What is Love? People have various genuine thoughts, beliefs, and experiences on this question. What can we gain from others? Those who want authentic Love need the depth ensured when adding God as number 1 to the mix. Communicating regularly with God adds so much to all our Loving human relationships. Having God always on our side in anything, especially Love, is a most incredible gift from God. Believe it and experience GOD!!! Other kinds of Loving relationships also occur without God fully involved. These are also authentic but not as strong as would be gained from God's involvement. (p.55)

Love is the ever-calling, ever-demanding, yet absolutely necessary aspect of our lives. The closer we are to God, the more robust and more realistic our Love for ourselves and others. (p.57)

Families are the necessary strength of any society. The stronger the family is in Love, the stronger the culture. Society needs to encourage and support strong, loving families and support those struggling and disadvantaged who need our help. We cannot ignore the calls from the poor! To ignore these is to not LOVE! We are always just one moment away from death! All of us must work, play, live, and love together within our community. (p.60)

Once someone knows and appreciates what true Love is, their whole approach to life, self, and others changes. Love changes all! (p.63)

Forgiveness is divine. (p.65)

True Love enables people to celebrate the successes of others. In this situation, the person who has achieved feels a sense of accomplishment and value, but the others feel happiness and joy. Loyal support. True LOVE. (p.67)

Why do decent human beings have an inherent desire to help others? Is it because it is universally the right thing to do? Is it GOD's Love carrying us forward? What about those who don't desire to help? (p.71)

The silent voice is an unheard cry from the needy, the poor, the ill, the weak, and the lonely. These people who have so little means are not heard beyond their immediate existence by the noisy, self-absorbed, selfish world. To show true Love, let us all commit to helping those in need in any way we possibly can. Let's start with those suffering and close to our own home – our families. (p.72)

TRUE LOVE True love means giving! True Love is not about taking! In times of absolute turmoil and destruction, true Love is seen as honest and visible. Love saves the day for many. (p.78)

Wisdom: GOD's Hints & Tips

We must stop believing that we are better than others! Share! Genuinely believe in each other! Assist! Love!!! Enjoy! (p.81)

Be prepared for the unexpected when praying with God. Trust in God and God's ways. Listen in your heart of hearts for that exceptional moment of communication with GOD. That particular message or feeling. That solution to help you through the tough times when GOD will be carrying you. (p.84)

Live a LOVING life, and LOVE will genuinely be there within you and with those you impact upon. (p.93)

I was one with nature - with a most remarkable, intelligent mammal - this wild but gentle, safe dolphin. Both of us enjoying each other at that one moment in time in our shared wave. (p.93)

Forgiveness of others and ourselves is often needed. (p.94)

Live a LOVING life, and true LOVE will be there for you from GOD!!! (p.94)

LOVE is so real. (p.94)

LOVE is the basis of life, and Love is from GOD! (p.94)

LOVE is the Meaning of Life. (p.94)

Nothing beats the bushland for spiritual balance and personal equilibrium. We all should have at least one bushland/watercourse place where we can go and feel 'at home' spiritually… All this comes about through the lifeforce each human, animal, and plant possess. (p.96)

GOD IS ABSOLUTE LOVE. We need GOD to have a genuine, authentic role in OUR LOVING lives. It is up to us to decide the answer to the big questions! Ask GOD for help with this decision-making! Nothing is forced by GOD! (p.99)

The new lifestyle is a simple one of loving the other as much as loving yourself. With God's help, this loving of the other is made easy - because it is so natural to do. So right to do. So important to do! (p.103)

I have discerned from GOD over many decades that...so many living creations, creatures, and flora alike must have a soul. These souls bring everything with life together as one. GOD is Life. God is Love. God is entirely with us throughout our Lives. GOD is ONE with US ALL. (p.106)

Pray to God. Listen to God. Do what God says. Enjoy GOD! (p.110)

It is from and with God that we genuinely experience Love. To share a genuine depth of Love with other people, we need God to be an integral part of this. God is Divine and Absolute Love! We need God through this highest level of Love. This is achieved through our prayer and the prayerful lifestyle we live. (p.114)

Be open to the unknown when exploring different prayer styles. Begin your prayer, acknowledging GOD being the number ONE of eternity and the universe. Truthfully ask God for forgiveness for your wrongdoings. Name these if you can. Forgive yourself as well. Then continue with whatever prayer format you are using that time. (p.114)

I realised how much more I should be doing. How much more I should be including God directly in my life. To see God as so crucial that multiple daily prayers are so strongly desired enhances our spirituality and closeness with the One God of this world. I gained so much understanding of prayer through the practice of Islam and two Islamic countries – Saudi Arabia and Bahrain. My local Imam back in Australia is a massive strength for Islam. (p.117)

The reason we want to live a fulfilled life comes from God out of God's ABSOLUTE LOVE and desire for our best. However, we cannot adequately appreciate this, as it comes from divinity, God, and we only have our humanity embrace and understand it as best we can. Generally, we have an intrinsic feel for this Love and these beliefs – and yearn for it before moving on to God at death! (p.123)

'Be Truthful' (First Revelation to Author in 2016) (p.125)

God loves us so much that we are all called to salvation with God in Heaven. We can't reject God!!! Too many believe all go to Heaven. God wants all to go to Heaven, yet whoever rejects God through their evil beliefs or lifestyles, etc., rejects salvation – outright! Except through a genuine life-changing request for forgiveness from God for their sinful rejection – right up to that God judgement at death. (p.127)

The most disappointing reality to all of this is that there are enough resources worldwide for all people to live faithful, comfortable lives EVERYWHERE. But all people, except the very poor, have to share their excesses and a considerable amount from their everyday accounts/lifestyle. Fairness isn't cheap! But justice is essential for true LOVE! (p.135)

Once we can forgive and be forgiven, we are set free. We can live more peaceful, fulfilling, and loving lives together. (p.144)

Bryan Foster

Let's encompass God fully! Let's live for Greatness - for God!!! Let's let God give us the time of our lives! Let's LOVE GOD honestly and allow GOD to LOVE US fully. (p.151)

The message is unambiguous – love each other as the ultimate lover, Jesus loved and loves. (p.153)

At this moment, in the Australian outback, at the public hospital in Katherine in the NT, I finally realised that you don't need much, just the necessities. This Gold Coast 'kid', who had become a middle-aged grandfather, had his values and priorities turned upside-down - to the correct position! (p.161)

My gasp was palpable and audible. I was stunned! I hurt for Billy (an elderly Australian First People) and his people. I was embarrassed at all I had and could have – from personal relations, professional opportunities, education, lifestyle, health and wealth, etc. I wanted to scream for Billy and his people! (p.162)

God is calling us to be in a unique oneness with 'Him'! Calling us to be unique yet an integral part of all humankind, and calling us to be human within God's loving embrace! That's GOD's REAL Love for each of us uniquely and together. (p.165)

Yes, this is quite raw emotion and nothing for which to apologise. The loving sentiment is the window to God. God gives the believers ways to know God is here. (p.178)

There is only one GOD – forever! And that there is no one single religion (yet)! All genuine religions have a crucial role in getting this new message of GOD today to their people. Ideally, a massive change religiously is needed as there is only a Need for One, True religion. All genuine religions need to combine, in time, like this – ONE RELIGION FOR ALL! By the book 6's Author. (p.181)

It is all up to the evil ones to turn to God and authentically request forgiveness and turn away from evil. If they can't, then that is their decision to end up existing in what they like best, as shown through their earthly behaviour, i.e., evil. Hell awaits them if they seriously accept evil as superior to Good. If they accept hate as being superior to Love. (p.188)

I have been deeply involved with the Catholic Church and Catholic schools for my whole life – over 60 years. My wife and two of our children are Catholic teachers. I was also for 42 years until retiring from teaching. Now I am writing religious and caravan/trailer travel books. In my time, I have only known priests, pastors, and religious brothers and sisters who want to do what is best for their communities. Nothing illegal or unethical. I am aware that there will be some who would say that I am biased (yet I would add - no more biased than anyone else who supports the Truth and follows the Truth given by God). Yet, for me to live within the Church for so long allows for a more complete understanding of the actual situation.

This is no rose-tinted appreciation – it is honestly real. (p.189)

Our One God of the Universe is there for EVERYONE - FOREVER. (p.191)

There is Only One Absolute Truth, and that is, and from, GOD. We have no right to interpret Truth as we please. If this was the case, there is no Absolute Truth, apart from whatever you want it to be! There is far too much criticism of GOD and religion based on the minimal literal appreciation of scriptures. The Contextual Approach to scriptural interpretation is essential to gain GOD's Absolute Truth Today. (p.207)

GOD is 'ALIVE' + DIVINE! GOD is One – Only One! For Eternity!

GOD Always Was, Is, and Will Be For All Time! (p.209)

GOD Is The Answer – Not the Problem (p.212)

When a person is open to GOD experiences, GOD will most likely become 'seen' or experienced to at least these aware people and maybe others around. Unless they deliberately turn away from GOD's presence and vigorously deny the existence of GOD, there should be some level of feeling or experiencing GOD's LOVE and PRESENCE. (p.213)

Listen and hear God's messages, God's people, and your personal experiences of God. God is the answer – not the problem! (p.213)

You can't change what exists just because you don't believe it + The Truth is the Truth, no matter what. GOD is GOD, no matter what. (p.215)

No matter how cynical the mainstream and social media and population may be, it is our duty from GOD, to tell the Truth for what it is… a massive challenge for a more and more GODless, western world! (p.215)

All the Justices of the Full High Court of Australia unanimously found Australia's Catholic Church leader innocent and had Cardinal Pell released from jail. (p.221)

Wisdom: GOD's Hints & Tips

As someone who has taught in Catholic schools for 42 years and who attended these schools as a student for a further eight years, I have never seen or heard from anyone at the schools I attended, or at the church where I was an altar boy, of being approached or harmed by any pedophile. Students and staff have spoken on numerous occasions about this possibility, but no one has experienced this in our local Catholic schools. (p.222)

Most of these anti-Church people come in two main categories. The first is the genuinely shocked members of our Church and community who are appalled at what happened and how it was treated by those in power, the clergy, and other religions.

The second is the GOD/religion/Church haters. (p.222)

Have no more fear of being a religious follower. You have GOD and the majority of the world on your side! Call for GODly or people's support when in need. LOVE GOD who LOVES you so MUCH that you could never imagine this level of LOVE is at all possible – but it IS and FOREVER?! (p.229)

There is no devil as such, but there is definitely considerable evil throughout this world. Sin occurs when WE choose to do something against GOD or GOD's teachings knowing this to be wrong. When this happens, the person is choosing - No GOD - for that moment in time. (p.236)

At the moment of a person's death, GOD will give each person one last chance to decide on GOD or no God - Heaven or Hell. Those who choose - no God - based on each person's former lifestyles and beliefs, etc. will be banished to Hell forever. (p.236)P

Our lives become enriched by living GOD's commandments and teachings. Primarily through loving others, in whatever form of Love, is dependent on the specific relationship. (p.239)

Following GOD can only make our lives more fulfilled, enjoyable, and rewarding. With the enormous bonus of heading in the correct direction to Salvation with GOD in Heaven. (p.239)

For those humans, animals, and plants that 'say', 'Yes', to GOD in GOD's divine ways, which are unknown to us humans at this stage, there will be eternal life with GOD and all those now heavenly souls/spirits in perfect harmony with GOD in Heaven. How the plants and animals relate and communicate with GOD is still a mystery? (p.243)

How would we react if Jesus, Mahomad, Moses, or Brahman walked into the room? Even in this world of so much of everything, yet becoming more of so little of GOD, I have a clue that people would initially freeze! Wonder? Question? Even challenge! Then most would rush over to do it [a selfie]!... (p.244)

'Tears from GOD' There is an overwhelming sense of GOD's Love and presence being intimately experienced at that moment.... it is very obvious to the recipient that it is on another level beyond the physical. Tears pour out in free flow. It isn't crying as we know it, but tears sent from GOD are flowing uncontrollably. (p.254)

Many people know that out of GOD's Absolute Love and our own Free Will, GOD, has to allow people to make bad choices with the various ramifications resulting. The answer as to why awaits us through our salvation with GOD in Heaven. We don't know when GOD will be calling us at death. Another mystery. (p.260)

The One GOD of the universe loves creation so much that no harm is desired on any person. Humanity is the pinnacle of living creations. Society has Free Will and the capacity to create or destroy our world. It's up to all of us!!! (p.261)

As a population, we certainly waste enormous amounts of money trying to look a certain way, be a particular type of person, have a specific image to maintain, gain various 'bonus points' from those we try to impress, etc. And all for what? (p.263)

God NEEDS us all to be as close as possible to GOD and each other - in true Love. GOD loves each of us so much. Absolutely. Forgiveness is essential for a Loving Life. LOVE NEEDS FORGIVENESS. FORGIVENESS BRINGS LOVE! (p.267)

The beautiful Muslim father who forgave his little son's accidental killer. An absolute inspiration for humanity! His Islamic faith is giving him incredible strength. (p.268)

Due to [Aayan Ali's] unquestionably lived experiences on both sides of the Reformation and Islamic argument, she will considerably help Islam achieve its desired peaceful outcomes. (p.272)

It is much more than just being peace-loving. It means placing GOD as Number One and allowing all our beliefs and values to permeate from GOD's teachings. GOD is the answer! Islam and Christianity both strongly support their religions and GOD/Allah when needed, and in the way, they do this. Islam is far more public, though, especially those from Islamic countries. Christians are generally quieter yet still very supportive in their ways and beliefs of GOD. (p.272)

We need GOD! We need what GOD offers all humanity equally. We need to accept God's unconditional Love for each one of us! (p.277)

I then started to get a message to write down what I was about to receive. I soon realised that, just as in ancient times, the mountain was a conduit to GOD. (p.313)

The need to accept my place in the scheme of GOD's plan and go and do whatever is required to propagate the Revelation or message! Each of these reasons supports the belief in either the Revelation or inspired messages. (p.324)

WISDOM QUOTES in GREY BOXES from the *'GOD Today' Series* –

GOD'S HINTS AND TIPS

Book 7

Wisdom: GOD's Hints and Tips (2021)

Each book in this *'GOD Today' Series* invites us in various ways to join in the discovery of GOD, GOD's Wisdom and Revelations, Inspired Messages and Love, as we journey towards our own personal and communal salvation with GOD on Earth and hopefully later in Heaven.

We must eventually accept that this relationship with GOD is the most positive, enhancing, honest, forgiving, and absolutely loving one we could ever imagine.

The closer we get to the Absolutely Loving GOD of Wisdom, the closer we can find out about our true soulful selves.

We find out that GOD's divine relationship with us all is so much more significant and impressive than for one we could ever imagine. (p.14-15)

GOD is just waiting for us to say,

'YES!'

'YES, I can!'

'Yes, I want You, GOD, to be a major and substantial part of my life.'

'Yes, I want to be a significant part of you, GOD's existence, too!' (p.38)

'I love GOD, and GOD loves me beyond anything I could imagine.'

The 'best-kept secret' is to LOVE GOD above everything else!!!

GOD is earnestly waiting for us to NEED 'Him' and work to be as close as possible to GOD! (p.38)

LOVE is from GOD.

GOD IS ABSOLUTE LOVE!

Everything we know about LOVE and its impact on us comes from GOD.

Every experience we have of LOVE is from GOD – and is of GOD with us.

It is GOD's ABSOLUTE LOVE encouraging us to grow together as One People, One World –

together with the One and Only, ONE-GOD for all religions!

Love is the Meaning of Life – GOD'S LOVE.

LOVE GOD!

LOVE EACH OTHER!

BRING EVERYTHING TOGETHER – as ONE. (p.39)

Mt Warning, New South Wales, Australia.
'Wollumbin' for the First Peoples.

Wisdom: GOD's Hints & Tips

GOD comes 'through' this mountain to the author with Revelations for propagating to as many people as possible.

The author's favourite in this *Series'* is BOOK 4.
Spectacular,
unique,
original images from GOD.

Jesus and Mahomad are both the one and only Incarnate GOD (GOD became human)
Of all time – past, present, future – of which we are so far aware. (p.75)

The world desperately needs true, genuine, authentic LOVE. The ONLY source of such Love is GOD!

Keep in regular contact with God!

Continually develop your Wisdom of Love.

Work to become much closer to, and with,

GOD through the – Wisdom of GOD's

Love. (p.111)

Revelation #15

Jesus is God [*]

Brahma/[n] is God

Yahweh is God

Mahomad/Allah is God [*]

[*] Don't doubt this

Bryan Foster

Mahommad is Allah is God

Jesus and Mahomad is God (p.117)

...[there is] the need to accept my place in the scheme of GOD's plan to go and do whatever is required to propagate the Revelations or Inspired Messages!

(Are you the reader also required?) (p.163)

...there was this incredible feeling of heat flow from my head downwards to my feet.

I then broke down and cried Tears from GOD - of absolute love for GOD and those around me.

This is the moment in time that all my confusion, doubts, and challenges about GOD disappeared. (p.169)

I then started to get a message to write down what I was about to receive...

I soon realised that, just as in ancient times, the mountain was a conduit to GOD. (p.173)

There is an overwhelming sense of GOD's love and presence being intimately experienced at that moment.

Words cannot describe what is happening... it is on another level beyond the physical.

It is not crying or sobbing as we know it, but tears incredibly, lovingly, flowing uncontrollably -

Tears from GOD. (p.187)...There was this incredible feeling of heat flow from my head downwards to my feet.

I then broke down and cried Tears from GOD - of absolute love for God and those around me.

Wisdom: GOD's Hints & Tips

This is the moment in time that all my confusion, doubts, and challenges about GOD disappeared. (p.187)

How can I experience GOD in special ways?

The following should hopefully enable you THE READER to see how you may be open to GOD's incredible LOVE and WISDOM. Pray to GOD. Listen to GOD. Do as GOD says.

GOD can share all these types of close associations with 'HIM' as GOD so chooses. People genuinely searching for GOD may at times also receive these Tears from GOD. There is no set plan to make this happen. It is up to GOD.

We can never put GOD to the test. We must wait and be ready for when GOD wishes for us to have these most incredible experiences of GOD's closeness, GOD's support, GOD's forgiveness, etc.

Those times when we authentically feel that GOD is carrying us figuratively across the negative times and challenges, which come our way throughout our lives. Carrying us to where 'HE' is and we want and desire to be with GOD. Openness to receiving GOD creates the most beautifull awareness for us to receive GOD when offered, in whatever way GOD wishes for this to occur. GOD leads. We follow. We learn.

These moments in time when GOD shares so much with each of us are those special and unique moments. Nothing on Earth or in our usual lives comes anywhere near these times. When the Truly Divine comes to each of us, we will know about it. We need to be prepared for this to happen. Be Open to GOD whenever you possibly can. It should then happen, if this is in sinc with GOD's plans for each of us.

CONCLUSION

Through our divine Creator, GOD's WISDOM is for all people for eternity and our acceptance of this for our developing Wisdom with GOD within our lifetime. Our relationship with GOD should move towards a special Wisdom from GOD for our Loving existence. Once our Wisdom from GOD is understood and developed, and accepted by each of us, our Love of GOD and people changes and grows into a unique, special bond. Our doubt of GOD, doubt of Truth from GOD, and doubt of goodness and holiness fade away. We begin to become one with GOD, grow with GOD, move towards our Love of GOD and feel GOD's incredible Absolute Love supporting and encouraging us on the remainder of our life's journey. Accept this Wisdom, and life will open before you to the open arms of our GOD.

Wisdom is the answer for everyone's Salvation with GOD after our life here on Earth. People who understand and appreciate GOD are developing their Wisdom of GOD, life, death, and Salvation with GOD. It is this Wisdom that brings people to GOD and Absolute Love. That gets people to Salvation with 'Him' in Heaven.

Understanding and appreciating GOD's Absolute Love and expectations of us becomes Wisdom for those people. To react to whatever Wisdom GOD passes to each of us brings us closer to our most loving GOD through our continually developing Wisdom over our lifetime.

GOD is the Absolute font of all Wisdom. GOD so much LOVES to share as much of this 'secret' saviour (Wisdom) as possible. It remains a 'secret' for many people who don't decide on the Loving direction to GOD. The 'secret' opens up and becomes a massive attraction for the GOOD/GODly people. It is the opposite for evil people, though. This growth towards both GOD and Heaven and a post-life of Absolute Love, Wisdom, and GOD, should be everyone's aim and direction throughout life. The 'door' of Heaven is open. Where are we on our travels to GOD and Heaven through this 'door'? Non-believers who totally reject GOD and GOODness don't even see the door to Heaven for which to aim. Anyone who deliberately and freely closes themselves off from GOD through their anti-God evil, beliefs and actions is Evil.

Knowing and loving GOD and knowing and loving yourself are essential for being one with GOD forever. Both these forms of Wisdom are critical for the world to turn to GOD FULLY. These wise earthly forms lead to the same path for all humans during their Earthly lives and their final Salvation with GOD.

Otherwise, their time after death will be swamped by Evil. Their choices are to be with the NO GOD side or totally and deliberately against GOD and therefore be with the EVIL existence of personal solitude in Hell forever. Absolute loneliness will be forever for these people who chose Evil and not God at that death moment.

As discerned from GOD, each person is given that one last chance at the instance of death – the choice is GOD or Evil! Each person at this stage will decide their future based on their lived lives on Earth before their death. A person who lived a sinful life, as their free choice for much of their lives, especially towards the end of their lives, when given the choice of Heaven or Hell, will most likely choose Evil/Hell because this is the lifestyle where they got most enjoyment in their lives, especially at their end-time of life. Until we get to Heaven, we can not appreciate these two options, and who decides which one of the two? Out of GOD's Absolute Love of humanity, each person is given their one last final choice at death – GOD/Heaven or Total Isolation/Hell? How this works, in reality, is another central mystery of GOD's. After death, it will become evident once we decide on Heaven or Hell, depending on our beliefs and behaviours at that last option given by GOD at death.

Another most surprising reality and still a divine mystery for us all, as discerned by the author from GOD, is that all living things, all flora and fauna, will be treated similarly to how humans have been judged over the millennia. It all comes back to how all lifeforms, and each individual within each lifeform category, treat GOD and GOD's teachings and place within the living world in whatever way they can do this. (There is also a place for lifeforms from throughout our universe and any other universe or existence of lifeforms eventuate.)

All lifeforms have souls (Lifeforms = soul) that exist in the way GOD chose. Souls are the life force present within all living fauna and flora, including humanity. Most of these beliefs may be possibly too difficult for many of the general population to appreciate or implement themselves? However, the closer to GOD we become, the clearer is the Salvation to Heaven of all soul-filled lifeforms here on Earth. People throughout eternity always have and may be able to appreciate this challenging reality as they prepare for a divine choice at death. Out of GOD's equal love for all, every person has the final choice of Heaven or Hell.

Why these Appendices?

These appendices assist with the background of GOD's Revelations and Inspired Messages and Bryan's pronouncement of these for GOD to today's world. Even though the lengths of a few are reasonably long, the included detail is essential for many readers.

The following appendices are aimed at those seeking more detail or a refresher from what has come before in this *Series* since Book 1 in 2016. It also covers those who are reading this book as their first within the Series.

Appendix 1
Highlighted Wisdom Quotes from Books One to Six - an Overview

* There is only One God for all religions, all cultures, for all time, forever.
* Jesus and Mahomad are both Incarnations of God who lived fully as humans before returning to be God in Heaven. (Revelation #15, 2016)
* Christian and Islamic leaders, theologians, and other scholars are called upon to explain #15 Revelation and how it applies to their religions and today's world.
* Islam has to reject violence, especially regarding the teachings about Mahomad's lifestyle and link to today's world.
* Tears from God, Revelations from God, Incarnations of God, etc., are essential background for the book's thesis and author articles.
* Islam and the secular world need new 'Reformations' and 'Renaissances' similar to the historical ones, due to corrections required worldwide. A world that is seemingly moving away from God.
* 21 Revelations to the author from God in 2016 and 2018 need implementing.
* Forgiveness is crucial for a loving world, loving countries, communities, families, and individuals.
* Prophets are genuine and need to be a part of our world. God works through prophets to highlight various Revelations. Find and support today's prophets.
* We NEED God so much today. Be open to God and God's ways. God is absolute Love, loving absolutely.

Wisdom: GOD's Hints & Tips

* Be aware of signs and coincidences from God. Examples of signs for this author are – sun rays, sun arrows, sun flares, double rainbows, and a colossal sun cross. The author believes these occur from God to encourage people to check and follow God's Revelations and messages, etc., as the Truth.

* Book 4 in the 'GOD Today' Series is a photobook of these signs from God. Some unique and challenging images indeed.

* The gifts of science and technologies are from God to us. These help explain the physical world, which should then help us all to use this knowledge from God for God's things for the world.

* God revealed 'Himself' to the author and gave humanity 21 Revelations for today.

* Mt Warning and its closeness to God for the author and his wife. It was on the plains of Mt Warning that God revealed the 21 Revelations for today's world.

* God loves each of us equally and absolutely and requires us to love God absolutely in return.

* Each day is a special gift from God of life. We live on a knife's edge and could live or die anytime, anywhere; this is God's choice.

*Why do we hang onto life so strongly when the possibility of being with God and living in perfection is what follows most people's lives here?

* Evil is real. Evil is when we freely decide to do, say, etc., against God's.

* People have one last chance to turn back to God on their deathbed. At that instance of death, God gives us one last chance to reject evil and love God.

* Evil people who can't change their ways and desire to continue to enjoy evil over good/God will end up in total isolation forever – in Hell!

* We need to share our God stories. People's closeness with God depends on their sharing with others and receiving these in return. The author's 26 stories in Book 1 (examples from over his lifetime) help set the parameters for each of us to see what our stories teach us about God, Love, forgiveness, etc. We should share our stories.

* Free Will – we all have this. We need to take this a step further and use it with our informed conscience to work out what God wants from and for us.

* Gifted, talented and fortunate people owe the world.

* Share the bounty. God requires each of us to do what we can for the poor, disabled, ill, disadvantaged, etc., people of our world. Greed is evil! Sharing legitimately is needed by all.

* All people on this earth can lead rewarding, fulfilled, loving lives if only the rich could share. Even those not wealthy but with more than needed are required to share. This is our only outcome when we know that God loves us all equally.

* Humans, animals, and plants all have a 'soul'. Soul=life. Along with a relationship with GOD and each other. (Discerned)

* Love and forgiveness are essential for authentic Love.

* Love is social justice for all.

* Humans feel the same inherently, until...

* GOD is Absolute Love

* We NEED GOD

* GOD makes life so much better when we allow this to occur

Wisdom: GOD's Hints & Tips

* Prayer is essential communication with GOD
* People desire to live a whole life so strongly. Then die to be with GOD.
* GOD can be found in relevant music and books
* Secularism is dangerous, hollow, and leading humanity to a catastrophe. A secular Reformation is also needed today.
* Media is relatively quiet on GOD. This must change quickly.
* Evil people must stop bullying and rejecting GOD and GOD's followers
* Former Muslim Ayaan Hirsi Ali, in her book, 'Heretic', 2015, calls on everyone to make Islam go through a Reformation, as most of the world has already done historically.
* Following GOD enriches humanity
* 'Tears from GOD' occur when someone is very close to GOD.
* Teachers and parents need passion and commitments to help adolescents grow towards GOD.
* Exemplify prayer for others. Show engagement with GOD.

** The spelling of 'Mahomad' by GOD in Revelation #15, plus once as 'Mahommad' when revealed to the author by God.

Bryan Foster

Appendix 2

What are the Revelations and Inspired Messages from God?

This book refers to Revelations as those inspired messages from God through a unique encounter with God and the person receiving them. However, there should also be some form of 'proof' of this reality, such as Tears from God and other justification points (explained shortly) before it is entirely accepted and shared as the Truth. Inspired messages are those thoughts and issues received through prayerful experiences or other people, nature, or events -from wherever God inspires us. However, a process of discernment is needed to clarify the authenticity of these and is different from ordinary thoughts and feelings.

The concept of 'Revelations' in this book is also referred to as 'Special or Direct Revelations' in various religious circles in society. God specifically directs these Revelations to individuals or groups. What is referred to as 'inspired messages' in this publication may, at times, be referred to as 'General Revelations' in other religious publications and discussions? These are from God to anyone in general, being received through such means as nature, ethical appreciations, and cognitive reasoning. (GCSE, BBC) Christianity believes that Jesus is the ultimate example of Revelation's fullness on this earth by humanity. (Oxford Scholarship, 2018) The different religions have various appreciations of the relevance of Revelations historically and today. All genuine religions believe that God reveals Godself to this world through various forms, especially through people, their beliefs and morality, and the natural world.

The terms 'Revelation' and 'inspired messages' are used as points of clarity. Naming every message God inspires humanity with the word 'Revelation' may become confusing as there are different Revelation levels. 'Revelation' is used when there is direct contact of God with specific people, while 'inspired messages' are for those revelations discerned by people as emanating from God. How both of these occur is explained.

Books 1, 3, and 5 primarily explain the various Revelations I received directly from God in 1982, 2016, and 2018, along with the inspired messages received from God and discerned over more than thirty-five years. There is an inherent, authentic sense of the Truth being shared.

The literary style states the Revelations and inspired messages received or discerned from God accurately without diminishing the emphasis of each through diplomatic, political, or politically correct forms.

The key Revelations and inspired messages will be stated clearly and without a softening or hardening to appease certain groups who may not fully or partially agree with each statement. Each Revelation and inspired message will be explained in enough detail to make the point succinctly and clearly.

There is a real emphasis on Keeping it Simple for God's People. This is a positive approach, not a negative one. Too often, religious preachers, teachers, and theologians emphasise too much detail beyond the message's clarity. People then get lost in all the detail, and the point from God is missed. In the 'GOD Today' Series, these books aim to keep the messages simple yet explained with enough detail to gain a proper understanding.

These books are not apologetic works. It is not teaching or preaching a set of one religion's doctrines over another religion's. It is not standing up and fighting for any particular religion or religious leader or any specific religion's specific beliefs or faith patterns.

Each is a Book of the Truth about and basically from the forever One and Only God of existence.

All genuine religions are equal and have an essential role from God for each of their followers. The belief in only one God is most liberating and beneficial for appreciating and following God.

This Truth is the Truth of God for today's global and interconnected world. The following section explains why I make this claim.

It has been quite a journey to get to this point. It began in 1982 when receiving the Tears from God and physical warmth flowing from head to foot received as part of the gift of healing from Sister Ann at a secondary school's Commitment Day where I was teaching. Over the interim period from 1982 until now, so much has been discerned as God's inspired messages. This discernment process is explained.

After receiving God's Revelation in 2016, explained in various ways and sections throughout the *Series* books, the initial reaction was one of doubt - even though there were many Tears from God on many occasions privately and with my wife, Karen, to show its authenticity and genuineness.

When it came to the crunch to decide what would be highlighted in the first book in this *'GOD Today' Series*, *1God.world: One God for All*, I wasn't able to run with all the Revelations. I only highlighted the 'One God Only – One God' Revelation and some subsequent discerned inspired messages from God and stories of experiencing God throughout my life. A real doubting Thomas scenario occurred. In hindsight, I now believe this was all part of God's plan. God initially wanted me to highlight the One God Only Revelation, along with the messages and stories contained in that edition.

This approach used for the first book in this *'GOD Today' Series* opened up the opportunities for me to grow into the other Revelations these past few years and to discern a better appreciation of each. To also gain the courage to go out into the world and state these with authority. It wasn't just a matter of listing these but to believe strongly in each one and explain each one in detail. God wanted these Revelations to become part of the world's meaningful and fully understood lexicon.

We all need to appreciate these Revelations and what these mean so that we can each make the Revelations an integral part of our lives.

Bryan Foster

How are the similar meanings of 'Revelation' words used in this Series?

Revelations appear to the receiver to be 'spoken' by God, through the 'mind's eye', (e.g., in the early morning hours for this author).

Inspired Messages are 'felt/experienced' as from God (e.g., most are eventually written down or seen as reflections by this author).

Vital/Key Points are primarily discerned and experienced, often over long periods, as being known to be the Truth from God and significantly add to the details being inspired by God. These are the 'everyday sort of information from God to whoever requires God's assistance.

(Edited Extract from *Where's God? Revelations Today*, 2018, by Bryan Foster, p35-38)

Appendix 3

Wise Revelations and Inspired Messages from GOD to Bryan Foster for Today's World.

GOD gave the author 21 Revelations in May 2016 (15) and November 2018 (6) for today's world. Both Revelations were given to Bryan around 3 am, at different venues near Mt Warning, Australia.

Referencing in this *Series'* books: Primary source = GOD. Secondary sources = books, websites.

There is ONLY ONE GOD for all people, all religions, all cultures, for all time - past, present, and future. (Rev. #10)

Jesus and Mahomad* are both Incarnations of GOD (* spelling as revealed by GOD to Bryan) (Rev. #15)

GOD IS ABSOLUTE LOVE (Discerned by author.)

GOD says that we are ALL EQUAL and LOVED EQUALLY by GOD (Rev. #9).

God's Revelations Book 3, # 1-21, Rev #1 to 12 (p.63ff.); Book 5, Rev #15 p.(118ff) Rev #16-21 (p.137ff.); Rev #6 (p.155); #13 (p.161); #14 (p.164f.)

1. Be Truthful
2. Don't be Greedy
3. Love life – don't take it
4. Respect all
5. Love one another as I have loved you
6. Die for what is right
7. Be educated for what is correct & truthful
8. Education is paramount for all

9. We are one
10. One God only – One God

> "I am a prophet Prophets are true" (This is close to the placement and punctuation in the Revelations received, i.e., after number ten and on the right lower side of the page. Is it referring to the author?)

11. God's messages to a world in need
12. This world is in enormous need
13. Cyberbullying – in all its forms, of all sorts, of all ages.
14. Fear rules – often from the cyber world eliminate this
15. God is Jesus & Mahomad
16. We need God
17. We need <u>to be vulnerable to God</u>
18. We need to continually be asking for God's help and assistance & support – always. 'No big heads' – Just ask for help. Always.
19. We are insignificant compared to God
20. God is so superior – face up to it. Believe it! Stop fighting it!
21. Be meek & humble & real

Revelations #1-15 from 29 May, 2016, received on the plains at the foot of Mt Warning, Murwillumbah Showgrounds, NSW Australia, after being awoken in the early hours of the morning while staying in my caravan/trailer.

Revelations #16-21 received at Mt Warning Rainforest Park @ approx. 3 am on 3 November, 2018.

Wisdom: GOD's Hints & Tips

The following few pages in Book 5 (p.137ff) explain each of the last six Revelations' discerned meaning, i.e., #16-21.

All Humans, Fauna and Flora are Soul-Filled and Divine at Birth! That's GOD's LOVE for all lifeforms on this Earth. (Discerned by author)

GOD desires for us all to go to Heaven at death. Yet we have the final choice decided together with GOD about where we will go – Heaven or Hell.

The Secular World needs a Reformation. GOD is highly NEEDED in today's world. (Rev. #11, 12, 16, 17, 18. Book 3 p.209ff)

Islam needs its Reformation – (See Ayaan Hirsi Ali, author of *Heretic: Why Islam Needs a Reformation Now*, 2015.) (Book 3, p.209ff)

Science is GOD's gift to humanity and the world. It is needed to help appreciate God's creations and then used to improve the world. (See Book 3, p. 195ff)

GOD's unique, photographic SIGNS were taken by the author for GOD to encourage people to believe that the Revelations and Inspired Messages, etc., shared by the author are from GOD, to assist them to believe in the Revelations, etc. gifted from GOD to Bryan. (See many unique and quite startling images in Book 4. See image explanations in Book 3 p. 148ff) These include sun arrows, rays, flares, a double rainbow, along with a giant Easter sun cross taken one week after Easter.

Each day is a gift from GOD. We need to treat it as such. We are called Home to GOD when GOD is ready.

Bryan Foster

'Tears from God' are gifts from GOD to help people realise GOD's closeness to them and that GOD's Revelations and Inspired Messages are authentic. (See Book 5, p.34, 82ff.) (There are enough examples seen worldwide and written about over the centuries for these to be genuinely real.)

GOD sent Bryan six Inspired Messages on the afternoon before the 15 Revelations were received on the following night in May 2016. (See Book 3, p113ff)

> GOD has permanent tears as from God;
>
> GOD is not the warrior image;
>
> but is the loving, caring, for all others;
>
> Our bodies are indeed the Temple of GOD;
>
> Purify [the body];
>
> Don't harm, poison it…illicit drugs, smoking

GOD seems to have invited the author to be a prophet and to espouse GOD's 21 Revelations. (See Book 5 p.20, 88ff) (The author is still discerning the legitimacy and reality of this invitation.)

Copyright © 2016-2021 Great Developments Publishers, Bryan (Author) and Karen Foster (Directors).

Appendix 4

Are the Wisdom Revelations and Inspired Messages contained in this Series the Truth from God?

Truthful, Genuine and Authentic Explanations

As an author, extolling the Revelations and inspired messages from God is a most challenging task. It goes well beyond my reflective writing of some thoughts and meanings. It goes to the whole core of appreciating ourselves, humanity, and our association with God. To claim the authority to do so is a massive personal challenge. Rest assured, it hasn't been done lightly. There is considerable truly heartfelt anxiety. *I genuinely believe in everything written in this publication wholeheartedly in my heart of hearts, soul of soul.*

The collection is one author's Revelations and inspired messages from God. Others throughout the world will also probably be receiving similar Revelations and inspired messages. Some may put these into publications. We all have our ways of dealing with and propagating what we receive. *All people can receive God's messages and Revelations.* The big question for each person is, Am I ready and open to receiving messages or Revelations from God? Would I know when I received any? What would I do with these if and when I had similar experiences to this author? God inspires us in so many ways, mainly through other people and nature. Am I aware of inspired messages from God through others and our world?

These Revelations and inspired messages revealed to me have been developing over at least forty years. It is not something that has just ensued. The culmination has been the 21 Revelations from 2016 to 2018 at Murwillumbah Showgrounds and the Mt Warning Rainforest Park in NSW, Australia.

The critical reasons for believing that these Revelations and inspired messages are from God are explained in more detail. The specific reasons below are followed by the detail of each subsequently.

- the 25th birthday experience and Revelation of God in May 1982 (Appendix 5);
- the Tears from God experiences, which have been growing in intensity and frequency, especially in the most recent years;
- the recent spectacular photographic images highlighting metaphorical or direct links with God;
- coincidences and signs from God over many years, especially in these past four years;
- the Revelations from God at the foot of Mt Warning in May 2016 and November 2018;
- the longevity without any personal doubt of my strong association with God;
- the personal career/vocation, 42 years teaching religion from years 1-12, including 30 years of Study of Religion to senior years 11-12;
- holding senior leadership positions in religious schools and parishes;
- prayer and meditation throughout and
- the continued strong support and agreement from my wife, Karen, and our families.

Wisdom: GOD's Hints & Tips

Each of these reasons supports the belief in either the Revelation or inspired messages being from God. God never forces anyone to believe anything. There is a level of 'proof' but also the mystery of the faith with any Revelation or inspired message from God. Therefore, through the combinations of these reasons and others, God's unique presence is experienced with the outcomes of each that needed to be shared. Having always been close to God, or at least in my teens on the fringes, allows for that openness to hear and know intrinsically when something is legitimately from God.

The 25th birthday experience is explained in detail in Appendix 5. I believe the longevity of living without any doubt about God since that 25th birthday experience is quite significant. Since that 1982 experience, when God came to many students, staff, and me on the schools' Commitment Day' is exceptional. The unique connection with God came about when prayed over by a charismatic religious sister/school principal who also had a master's degree in psychology. There has been absolutely no doubt about God's existence or God's absolute equal love for each human person throughout history. This 1982 revelatory moment was when I first truly experienced Tears from God in such depth. It also included the incredible warmth flowing from Sister's hands placed on the top of my head downwards through my whole body.

From that moment, over thirty-five years ago, there have been some tough and challenging times, as there are for everyone over their lifetimes. For me, these were mainly of personal health and financial types. Some were life-threatening or life-changing beyond any expectation or plan.

There was also the average life challenging experiences of others. These range from family to global. The global challenges needing to be worked through include war, poverty, and other injustices throughout the world and God's place with all these. Then there are the direct challenges in your beliefs, particularly from atheists. Members of this group are becoming particularly vicious and hate-filled towards anyone who espouses faith in God. You have to wonder why this is their form of defence/attack? There must be something more – do they feel guilty? Insecure? Ignorant? Unloved? Intellectually challenge? I just so wish they could be open and deliberately give God a go. We have to challenge these people out of love for God and the Truth. Stop hiding from the Truth. The Truth will set you free!!! For me, this hateful reaction was experienced directly when I opened myself up to various religious sites on social media to introduce my first *GOD Today' Series* book, *1God.world: One God for All in 2016*.

The Tears from God's experiences have been growing in intensity and regularity in recent years. (See p.52ff, 124ff for greater detail.) These were initially experienced in 'introductory' levels from about fifteen in year ten when I first wondered if I would like to join the priesthood, through to a higher level while at College in my late teenage years. One significant and influential event while at College was visiting a Sunday night charismatic mass where people were being healed through the Holy Spirit. The 25th birthday moment was the first significant Tears from God moment for me. Since then, similar sorts of occasions have been potent and enhancing. Each shows those extraordinary moments of pure bliss and the presence of God.

Wisdom: GOD's Hints & Tips

The Tears from God are the primary means of knowing God's unique presence and occasion of confirming those Revelations or inspired messages.

In 2016 at the foot of Mt Warning, I was awoken and told by God in my mind's eye to write down precisely as God sent me the Revelations. The 3 am early morning encounter with God is in the 'Mt Warning…' story throughout this *Series*. This supernatural Revelation was confirmed the following morning at a First Communion Mass in the nearby church where I married Karen forty-two years ago this year – through a Tears from God moment. Once again, two years later, more Revelations occurred at the foot of Mt Warning. These are those numbered sixteen to twenty-one.

There have been some different experiences, often recorded as photographs and featuring the sun, which shows God telling a story or offering a particular message. This message may be metaphorical or literal. Often it is God giving a sign of support or confirmation of that specific message. A point of encouragement to the message's authenticity and the need for it to be shared with others. In my particular case, the need to accept my place in the scheme of God's plan and to go and do whatever is required to propagate the Revelation or message is also a genuine aspect!

In 2018 there were five quite similar sunlight events to each other, in close time proximity. One occurred at the foot of Mt Warning just after sunrise, another at Texas on the NSW/Queensland border, a third was at Straddie, North Stradbroke Island. In contrast, another two occurred at Kingscliff and Cabarita beaches in northern New South Wales, close to Mt Warning, Australia. I believe that these images are part of the overall methods God uses to make particular points. These are just one method of many, though.

Coincidences and signs often point to special moments. In *Where's God? Revelations Today Photobook Companion: GOD Signs (2nd ed)* these are explored along with previously mentioned various sunlight experiences. Many of the images seem so incredible. Some might even wonder if the photos had been enhanced. Not so, though. One exception, though, is the image of Mt Warning with a small cloud atop its peak. The image needed different colours to give genuine authenticity to that photo's sun's rays emanating from the cloud and travelling outwards and upwards.

The chosen career/vocation choice to teach and specialise in teaching religion eventuated forty-two years of teaching religion in religious schools. Needing and strongly desired, starting each school day and each religion lesson with God's communication is incredibly empowering. Class prayer and meditation were highly significant for all these years. For thirty of these years, the academic Study of Religion classes for years eleven and twelve required the spiritual dimension and the academic dimension. This subject needed an intimate knowledge and considerable experience, if possible, of the various religions of Christianity, Islam, Judaism, Buddhism, Hinduism, and Australian Indigenous Spirituality. Teaching religion on these multiple levels every working day for such an extended time develops a genuine spiritual relationship with God. A truly loving relationship with the Divine! Your day is so much God-based. You truly get to appreciate God from each religion's perspectives and beliefs. Combine this with your own daily prayerful and meditative relationship with God, and a teacher of religious faith has something exceptional and unique from which to share.

Senior leadership positions in schools and parishes help with developing your relationship with God. These positions resulted from the personal, academic background being based on Theology, Scripture, Liturgy, and Religious Education, from experience gained in schools, and through the personal spirituality being shared. Each qualification up to a master's degree has multiple levels of religion covered. Whether you are leading a school as principal or leading the religious school's religious aspect as an assistant principal or senior school levels as a Year Coordinator, you should exemplify and live your relationship with God, your faith, and beliefs. You are challenged daily with everyday human aspects of others' relationship with God, religion, the religious school, etc. Through all this, your relationship with God grows and strengthens.

Senior parish roles result in similar experiences to the religious school but on a parish or deanery level. A deanery is a geographical grouping of various local parishes. It is led by the leadership priest, who is known as a Dean. In my roles of Chair or Secretary of the parish or deanery pastoral councils place you as a non-clergy leader, primarily of both the service and visionary aspects. You are there to help facilitate your parish or deanery members' spiritual, religious, and pastoral growth as a laity help for the priests. Through experiencing the challenges and best of all these people you deal with through these roles, you cannot help but be strongly influenced by their challenges, successes, and failures in life and their relationships with God and each other. The influence this has on strengthening your relationship with God is substantial.

When you have an authentic, prayerful relationship with God, so much of God's truth becomes apparent for these faithful. The impact is positively life-changing. You so much trust in God. God helps you through good and bad times. You have genuine compassion and empathy for humanity. God is indeed central to your existence.

The commandment about placing God as Number One across all genuine religions becomes accurate and actual. You then naturally aim to love each other as God does. It is through this prayer, meditation, and action for God's lifestyle (as exemplified by Jesus, God Incarnate) that you are more open to God and more prepared to discern God's messages for yourself and others. Discernment of God's Words becomes not just natural but an essential part of your life.

Karen, my wife of forty-two years, this year is integral to my relationship with God. Karen adds a depth needed to encounter God in these unique ways. She helps me understand and appreciate God's messages and Revelations through her unwavering support and openness to discuss each moment, each experience, each Tear from God encounter. And to share her contacts, often as the necessary support for my interaction with God!

(Edited Extract from *Where's God? Revelations Today*, by Bryan Foster, 2018, p. 39-45.)

...[there is] the need to accept my place in the scheme of God's plan and to go and do whatever is required to propagate the Revelations or Inspired Messages!

(Are you, the reader, also required?)

Bryan Foster

Appendix 5

Where the Wisdom for the '*GOD Today*' Series all began – Author's 25th Birthday Revelation

The day doubt disappeared, and my faith journey went to an unimagined higher level. On this day, I gained a whole new perspective of GOD and GOD's part in my life. Tears from GOD's love were experienced for the first time. The doubt about the reality of GOD disappeared. 'Let Go and Let GOD' became an actual spiritual reality of a profound order.

The stars all seemed to have aligned. It was my 25th birthday. As well as the school's uniquely offered annual 'Commitment Day'. It was also my last day at this school. At the end of the day, I left this school for my first country school principalship – which began on the Monday after leaving Brisbane.

It started with birthday excitement but the last day of school sadness and ended in tears of absolute joy and oneness with GOD.

This school was unique in its philosophy and enrolment policy. One key difference to most schools was their strong association with the charismatic Catholic movement. This was especially manifested in the annual 'Commitment Day' to GOD. Various staff had special gifts from GOD, which they actively used within the charismatic movement, but are not limited to this movement. Many people have these multiple gifts from GOD but often aren't aware of such gifts. The other common one is Speaking in Tongues, which I have witnessed on many occasions. On this day, the seven teachers with the charismatic gift of healing were engaged for much of the time, healing students and teachers alike. This healing encompasses any weaknesses we have, e.g., physical, emotional, or social.

On this day, the students and staff of this junior secondary Brisbane Catholic school began the day with a special Mass celebrated by a charismatic priest from Melbourne. The mass was followed by an invitation to students and staff to commit to GOD sometime throughout the day. There was no compulsion, though. The students could roam the school freely throughout the day, with the only prerequisite being no noise near the church. Staff supervised.

The staff of fourteen had seven charismatic teachers who had the spiritual gift of healing. One of these, the principal, was a sister in a religious order. Many of these charismatic teachers, plus the priest, presented at various positions within the church throughout the day. Students could choose who they would like to pray with when offering their commitment to GOD. Most stations would have many students continue with the staff member.

I sat with a particular student during the mass. This student was in a few of my classes. It took about an hour after mass concluded for this student to ask me to accompany her to pray with the principal and her present group of students. It was quite an event to go through the process of getting there due to various circumstances. However, once there, we were invited by the principal to move to the front of her group of eighteen to twenty students. Sister asked this student if she would like us to pray for her. She then asked me if I'd like to place my hand on the student's shoulder and pray. I agreed and prayed for her from very deep within my heart and soul - no speaking in tongues, just everyday English.

This belief in prayer causing healing, however, had caused me significant challenges that morning. I was tearing myself apart inside through the doubt that enveloped me about the whole healing circumstances that had been occurring in the church that past hour. Not being a charismatic person and having significant doubts about the entire healing process through a person being prayed over action caused me significant concerns. Much of this doubt was based on the television evangelists we would see on Sunday morning television back in the 1970s and 1980s, where people were miraculously 'healed' in large numbers before our very eyes as if this was the norm. There was truth to many of these healings, yet there was always so much doubt, as well. It was remembering that many of these tele-evangelists eventually admitted to fraud or other inappropriate behaviours. I had also witnessed charismatics healing at a local Brisbane parish while eighteen years of age and at teachers' college. This had impressed me enough to want to consider it more. The tele-evangelists over the previous years until this Commitment Day made belief in this healing process very difficult indeed.

So, as I walked this young lady to Sister, I was in incredible anguish internally. I was fighting against the possibility of something extraordinary. Each group had crying or sniffling people, and all were arm in arm with each other. It seemed to be too much for this doubter. Once I was asked by Sister to pray for the young lady, I instantly decided to 'Let Go and Let GOD'. This freeing moment was something quite unbelievable in itself. The confusion and doubt turned to belief and love. Sister then placed her hands on the girl's head and prayed. At that moment, the student broke down, and tears freely flowed. I was now also tear-filled.

Wisdom: GOD's Hints & Tips

Next, Sister asked if I'd like her to pray over me. What followed was life-changing. As she placed her hands on my head and prayed, there was this incredible feeling of heat flow from my head downwards to my feet. I then broke down and cried tears of absolute love for GOD and those around me. This is the moment in time that all my confusion, doubts, and challenges about GOD disappeared.

Later that afternoon, I asked Sister what had happened, and she explained that GOD came into me and that my old self was 'washed away' (downwards) and that I was 'filled up' with the new me.

I have remained so faith-filled and full of GOD's oneness and awe ever since – that is 36 years. My faith has never wavered since that day, even when some very challenging issues have confronted me. GOD was with me through each of these.

That was the day I truly learned that tears in specific instances are a sign from GOD - that GOD is truly present at that particular moment.

I am often asked if a similar experience of how GOD came to me, along with the Tears from GOD, will happen to others, to my students, their families, and friends, my colleagues, etc. I genuinely believe that it could if the opportunity availed itself. We need to accept GOD's offer, whenever and wherever made. We may need to search out the possibilities. We may not expect it when it does happen. I believe the secret is always to be open to receiving GOD in both expected and unexpected ways. GOD loves us beyond our imagining and wants the best for each of us. We must not be blinded to GOD by all the distractions of this world. We need to be prepared for GOD to come in whatever way GOD chooses. It may not be what we expect, though.

We need to clear our minds and hearts to the beauty, purity, and awesomeness that is GOD. We need stillness, openness, and desire to accept whatever GOD offers, whenever GOD provides it.

The notion in much of the western world today is that we don't need GOD. It is either because we have so much or because we are blinded by so much - which is an absolute fallacy.

We need GOD as much today, if not more than at any time and at any place in history have needed GOD.

It is the first significant time in history that the belief in GOD and acceptance of GOD being with us on this earth is diminishing. It is a time of absolute urgency requiring a major cultural shift towards GOD and GOD's people here today.

(Edited Extract from *Where's GOD? Revelations Today*, 2018, by Bryan Foster, p131-135)

…there was this incredible feeling of heat flow from my head downwards to my feet.

I then broke down and cried Tears from God - of absolute love for God and those around me.

This is the moment in time that all my confusion, doubts and challenges about God disappeared.

Bryan Foster

Appendix 6

Mt Warning/Wollumbin – Word of GOD Revelation – the Wisdom Story

In 2016 GOD 'came down' from the mountain. This most majestic Australian 'mountain' in the Northern Rivers, NSW, and offered forth a most remarkable experience of GOD for the author. Having just spent three days touring around Mt Warning, reflecting on it, photographing and videoing it, and staying in a caravan/trailer park on its plain, all was to culminate in a nighttime oneness with GOD event. This Revelation moment is indelibly etched on my whole being.

I had the most remarkable opportunity to experience GOD's Word firsthand, literally. I had taken leave to recuperate from illness and stayed for a few days in a caravan in my wife's original hometown. The campsite I chose significantly had a view of Mt Warning in the background. A 'mountain' I had viewed thousands of times over the years, mainly since I was 18, met my future wife and local farming family. Mt Warning is an imposing 'mountain' feature in the far north of New South Wales, Australia. I say mountain; in reality, it isn't in any comparative height sense like Europe/Asia or the Americas. For the oldest continent on Earth, Australia, it is quite imposing. Being a volcanic core, it stands out literally within the caldera features of a vast ancient volcano. The shape is very appealing and attractive. Its centrality within the region causes it to be a feature admired from all directions.

Over three days, I drove the 72km around its base and up to the walkers' departure point (on bitumen and gravel roads). Around sugar cane farms and through national parks and small villages, I videoed and photographed it from all possible directions, sat and reflected with it, observed it, drove and walked to crucial observation points, visited its base, and became very familiar with it. You could almost say I became one with it.

On the third day, I was awoken at night. I was very aware of my breathing and of breathing cold, fresh, clean air. I just lay there breathing deeply in through the nose, holding each breath for a couple of seconds and slowly blowing it out through the mouth. There was a real sense of presence. I started to realise it was quite a cold night and that I was lying at the foot of Mt Warning, relatively. I began to get this powerful awareness that I was one with the mountain. The mountain and I had grown together significantly these past three days, and now we were at a climax. The Truth would become apparent.

I then started to get a message to write down what I was about to receive. And to be very accurate.

I soon realised that, just as in ancient times, the mountain was a conduit to GOD. Prophets from many religions had climbed mountains closer to GOD and received GOD's message for that time and place in history and often for subsequent eras. I was not to climb the mountain tonight. (Or ever again due to an injury.) But I was to climb it figuratively.

Or was it a case of GOD coming down from the mountain?

Remarkably, what followed blew me away! Without thinking about what I was to write, I found myself writing down a list of instructions, teachings, and refreshers. Was it indeed from GOD? It sure felt like it. But how could I tell? I was told within my mind not to overthink this, to go with the flow - that it was all legitimate and would become apparent as the night went on. The challenge for me was that since my 25th birthday religious experience (See 25th birthday story in Appendix 5, p.196ff), tears were a sign for me of GOD's presence; the more significant the tears, the greater the divine presence. (See 'Tears from GOD')

Yet, there were no tears tonight. But there was ecstasy and a realisation of what was happening. A font of wisdom was unfolding, and I was so, fortunately, a part of it. The list was completed. An explanation from me of what had occurred was recorded after the list. (See 'Revelation Notes' after the 'GOD's 12 Revelations' section.) And a perfect sleep followed.

The following day was a Sunday, and I attended the Catholic sacrament/ritual of the Eucharist in the church in which Karen and I were married forty years ago this year! The mass was by coincidence a First Communion Mass for the local Catholic school. During the Mass, I asked GOD if what happened last night was real – what followed was an outpouring of tears. The answer was an emphatic, "Yes!"

(Edited Extract from *Where's GOD? Revelations Today*, 2018, by Bryan Foster, p58-60)

Wisdom: GOD's Hints & Tips

I then started to get a message to write down what I was about to receive…

I soon began to realise that, just as in ancient times, the mountain was a conduit

to and from

God.

Appendix 7

Tears from God – One of GOD's Signs of Wisdom showing 'His' Divine Presence

My 'Road to Emmaus' experience, my epiphany, the 'Commitment to God' day on my 25th birthday highlighted something extraordinary from God.

It became evident that when God wanted me to know something exceptional was coming from God, there would be passing on the Tears from God. These are not God's tears physically, but these are tears from God spiritually, which I experience physically, emotionally, and spiritually.

There is an overwhelming sense of God's love and presence being intimately experienced at that moment. Words cannot describe what is happening, as it is evident to the recipient that it is on another level beyond the physical. Tears pour out in free flow. There is no everyday contorted facial expressions or sobbing, as is typically associated with crying. It isn't crying as we know it, but tears are flowing uncontrollably.

Many others also experience these Tears from God. No one religion can claim this existence solely, as it occurs across several religions. This section mainly looks at the place of the tears in Christianity, Islam, and Hinduism.

Just as these Tears overwhelmed me all those years ago, each time God needs me to realise that something extra special is happening, or that differentiation is necessary between the things of this world and the things God wants me to know about or do, or that I need strong support as part of God's plan, God shares the Tears.

Wisdom: GOD's Hints & Tips

Many will say that this is all just emotion and that the tears come because I am emotional about something. Early on, this was my thought too. However, over time, there has developed a clear appreciation of the difference between normal emotional tears and those from God.

The difference is difficult to explain, other than to say that the recipient gets this inherent feeling simultaneously as the Tears that God is making it known that God is uniquely present at that moment. It is not just like *feeling* God's presence but *knowing* God is present.

Sometimes you almost hear words from God, but you know these are your words being inspired by God. Many people would appreciate this from their own prayer life when messages come to them from God. It is God's inspiration but through your thoughtful words.

These Tears from God were called on several times as I went through these books' development. I needed to be continually reminded that the Revelations and inspired messages of the books were correct. In *1God.world: One God for All* it was especially needed for the central premise and Revelation being unconditionally accepted before it was published: that there is only one God for all religions, peoples, and cultures - forever. As well, all the inspired messages within the book up until the Mt Warning Revelation experience had been discerned as correct over several decades, yet reassurance through the Tears from God was still needed before publication. Similar support and verification from God were required for the following books, *Where's GOD: Revelations Today (2018)*, *Jesus and Mahomad are God (2020)*, and *Love is the Meaning of Life: GOD's Love*

(2020/1) with the publication of the Revelations and inspired messages contained within.

With the initial planning done in May 2016 for the first book, it was time to get God's approval. I stood with my wife, Karen, in our kitchen one evening and let her know I wasn't sure of the central premise for publication being singled out and emphasised, as I hadn't had any confirmation message from God. I was concerned that I might have been overstepping the mark. At that moment, a rush of tears filled my eyes – Tears from God answered my call! The message from God was palpable - that it was correct and to go ahead, write the book, and publish.

Since that time, there have been various other occasions when this assurance has been given, especially at Mt Warning. One particular example evolved into a video of this topic being recorded with Mt Warning as a background. **

I realise many people will challenge my belief in this. However, all I can say is that I inherently know it is correct and that I have God's support and encouragement to state this publicly and emphatically. (See also the 'Revelations and Inspired Messages from God' Appendix 1, p.261ff and 'Are the Revelations…the Truth from God?' p.110ff)

Let us consider where the Tears from God historically come from when considered in the three example religions of Christianity, Islam, and Hinduism.

Christianity has long believed in this phenomenon, often referred to as the 'gift of Tears' from the Holy Spirit (God). The Holy Spirit freely gives charismatic gifts. Ewing beautifully encapsulates the closeness with God caused by these tears when she highlights how the Holy Spirit is infused into the receiver's soul. The tears' action is the physical sign and personal experience of this bringing about such a result. The person will often be unable to explain what is or has happened - that the experience is somewhat subconscious and in a different realm.

Fenelon states how Pope Francis refers to these as 'the gift of Tears'. He emphasises how this helps prepare the receiver to see Jesus (God) and how the concept is based on the 'Spiritual Exercises' of St Ignatius, especially where Ignatius is overwhelmed by the consolation of God. The Tears are coming from a sense of deep intimacy with God, primarily while Ignatius celebrated the Eucharist in all its beauty and presence of God's love. She goes on to share theologian Tim Muldoon's thoughts on how the pope sees this as a mystical experience of a deep, preconscious conviction of God's presence. It results from an overwhelming experience of receiving God's intimate love, which can only be expressed through the free-flowing tears.

Fr Bartunek, an evangelical Christian and is now a Catholic priest, explains that this gift can occur singularly or on multiple occasions. He states that it doesn't mean the receiver is any holier or closer to God than others. He says it is an event to encourage those receiving or witnessing it to be in more significant and more substantial relationships with God. It provides excellent comfort from God or confirming decisions they had previously made and defense against temptation.

Physiologically, Bartunek notes how these Tears from God are not like healthy tears, resulting in sobbing due to everyday life's emotions. Still, these tears flow abundantly and freely without any physical tension or facial contortions. He also mentions that this gift isn't in scripture or the Catechism but has been referred to by various spiritual writers since the early Church.

In Al-Islam, examples of Tears from God are seen in both the Qur'an and traditions. Some examples in the Qur'an include when Tears occur as a sign of perceiving the realities of God or as a sign of wisdom. Prophets shed tears for Allah when hearing of communications from God. Tears are seen as so significant in Islamic tradition that they are a gift to humanity, illuminate and soften the heart and bring about a great reward from God, including extinguishing God's wrath.

Rattner speaks of what he calls the emotion of devotion, a crying for God, which he explores from the Hindu and Christian traditions. Like both the Christian and Islamic examples above, the Tears come from God at those special and often unique transformational moments with God. These were regular and spontaneous, purifying him to experience higher conscious states, leading to continual spiritual development.

** See 'Tears from God…' video at - https://www.youtube.com/watch?v=z5mmNvIKko4…t

Appendix 8

Peacefulness with GOD – a deeply personal experience

Early this year (15/04/2021), I headed for the Murwillumbah Showgrounds after packing up the caravan at the Chinderah caravan park, Tweed Heads, where I stayed for a few nights to work on this Book 7.

As I began the drive from the campsite, I experienced an immense feeling of enormous peacefulness, Love and tranquillity. It was a calmness of exceptional Love. This I cannot recall happening at a similar level since my 25th birthday experience. I had peaceful and Loving incidents when GOD gave me the 21 Revelations in 2016 and 2018. But these were somewhat different.

So, my trip this morning was incredibly peaceful and quiet, *with a tremendous feeling of Love – Perfect Love from GOD.* As I moved through this experience while driving from caravan park to showgrounds, the feeling became incredibly unique and outstanding. It was a most pleasurable, peaceful, forgiving one. So much so that I seriously considered having a forgiving, reconciliation time directly with GOD. I therefore did.

It was so powerful that I wondered where it was going to take me. Now I feel like it may be how you feel when going back home to GOD (Heaven). It was so Loving and 'calling' that I seriously thought of the major conclusion to whom this may introduce me while driving along the highway. However, this was not to be so. I am still here and still writing for GOD. That serious and authentic Loving feeling I received from GOD earlier this year now continues with me. I just Love it!!! So hopefully will you too. Be open to GOD in everything we do.

> That serious and authentic Loving feeling I received from GOD earlier this year -
>
> now continues with me.
>
> I just Love it!!!
>
> So hopefully you will too.
>
> We need to be genuinely open to GOD in everything we do.

Appendix 9

GOD's Powerful Signs and Coincidences

Coincidences??? (See Book 4 in *the 'GOD Today' Series*, i.e., *Where's GOD? Revelations Today Photobook Companion: GOD Signs*, for explanations of unique, exceptional, and challenging photographic examples of GOD's signs and coincidences, which I was extremely fortunate to receive. It is my favourite book in this *Series*.)

The showground is where you can see Mt Warning in the not far distance. These showgrounds are on the plains of the Mt Warning/Wollumbin, northern rivers of NSW, Australia. It was here that I received the first 15 of the 21 Revelations in 2016. I was on the same camping showground's site when this was article was originally written, in 2021, as I was in 2016.

Some coincidences based on the number 25 with spiritual overtones follow. Once these sorts of coincidences are experienced and acknowledged as reality, it is one method that opens the possibilities for all folk alike also to have or finally accept similar experiences. Why? Does it sound too outright to say that if I, as an ordinary man, can receive these, why can't others? I passionately believe that they can. This is how GOD often works. Those who are open to assist GOD as disciples/followers, or who will become this way over time, will most likely have an opportunity to do so at some stage in their lives.

The coincidences were:

1. On arrival at the showgrounds, I was offered and accepted **site 25** from the park's manager.

Coincidence? The number 25 has significant significance for me ever since my 25th birthday. Coincidence or Gift from GOD? This site was where I received the Revelations from GOD #1 to #15 of the 21 in 2016.

2. On my **25th birthday** in 1982, several coincidental events occurred on the one day. The most significant was when I first received the **'Tears from God'** while being prayed over by the secondary school's principal, Sr Ann, at Seton College's 'Commitment to God' day. I also had more minimal tears from GOD during my school days, when I was considering entering the priesthood, from years 10 and 11.

3. It was the exact day I **left the first secondary school** in which I taught.

4. This required moving my family, Karen, my wife, and our first daughter, aged four months, **to Tara** in southern country Queensland. **We left late that afternoon.**

5. It was on the College's unique **'Commitment to GOD' Day**. This is the only school that celebrated this, of that I am aware. Sr Ann was a charismatic healer, as were another six out of the fourteen teachers on staff. The day commenced with a Eucharistic Liturgy (Mass), celebrated by a charismatic priest from Melbourne, Victoria.

The rest of the day was turned over to the opportunity for students and staff to freely commit to GOD in a unique and public way, if they so desired. This may have occurred anytime throughout the day. Students were free to roam throughout the campus, except those around or close to the church needed to respect the quietness – which they did brilliantly. (More details on this 25th birthday story from Seton College may be found in Appendix 5, p. 167ff in this book in *'GOD Today' Series*.)

6. **Sr Ann prayed over me** after I eventually **'Let Go and Let GOD'** occur. Until that moment, I was fighting its possibility. There was much to doubt, especially after various television shows were viewed on its healing activities from other countries. The shows seemed way too unreal and quite disingenuous, at times, for many of us. The fundamentalist approach (belief in the Bible literally) seems too un-Australian for most. It isn't easy to get a handle on it. (As an example, most Australians would happily be contextual, i.e., understanding and appreciating the Bible in its most profound sense. Interpreting the Bible contextually and figuratively.)

There was quite a physical reaction from Sr Ann's laying on hands after offering me the opportunity to receive GOD in an exceptional way. It was so real. Getting a handle on it is now complete. I fully believe now that GOD does come to people in extraordinary ways. As she placed her hands on the top of my head, immediately **an incredible warmth appeared inside me and travelled from head to feet**. Extraordinarily **serene and peaceful** was the occasion. Quite quickly, I started to cry, **Tears from GOD**. These were not normal emotional, sobbing tears but extra unique God-given signs and experiences. GOD came to me in a special and remarkable way.

7. This was my last day at Seton College. I had resigned from the College to move to **Tara, as their Catholic primary / elementary school principal**.

I left Seton that day surrounded by a sense of absolute Love of GOD and GOD's creations, human and other life forms. Along with an experience that had already changed my life. I Love GOD so much now that I have not had any negative thoughts about GOD or GOD's ways and expectations since that unique, extra special DAY – my 25th birthday, 39 years ago.

Warning!

Too many people have this incorrect appreciation of Good and Bad and its various outcomes.

Following GOD is good.

Following Evil is terribly bad.

People who think ignoring GOD's guidance by doing whatever they feel like,

no matter how stupid,

hurtful to self and others, and wrong, etc,

all in the name of fun;

is somehow good for them?!

GOD only offers

Love.

Love of all people who have, are or will live.

And a Love of all creation.

There is an overwhelming sense of God's love and presence being intimately experienced at that moment.

Words cannot describe what is happening… it is on another level beyond the physical.

It is not crying or sobbing as we know it, but tears incredibly, lovingly, flowing uncontrollably -

Loving Tears from the Loving God.

Bryan Foster

Author's Websites

https://www.GODtodayseries.com/
-- Main website for this Series, includes the regularly updated blog commenced in 2016

https://www.jesusandmahomadareGOD.com/ - Book 5 (Coming Soon)

https://www.bryanfosterauthor.com/- Author's website

https://loveisthemeaningoflifegodslove.com (Coming Soon)

https://loveisthemeaningoflife.com (Coming Soon)

http://www.greatdevelopmentspublishers.com/ - Publisher's new webpage. (Original website started in 2007, closed 12/2018. New webpage now.)

https://www.facebook.com/groups/389602698051426/ - 1GOD.world Facebook

https://au.linkedin.com/in/bryanfoster - LinkedIn

https://www.youtube.com/user/efozz1
- 780+ YouTube videos commenced in 2009. Themes - 'GOD Today' Series. Caravan/trailer hints and tips for beginners. Places to see and things to do, mainly in Australia.

Tears from God...' video at -
https://www.youtube.com/watch?v=z5mmNvIKko4

https://twitter.com/1GODworld1 Twitter

Instagram (1GODworld) (Development stage)

Index

1, 98, 171
1 God, 98
1God.world, 16, 31, 32, 148, 174, 187, 192
Absolute Love, 36
acting, 6
Australia, 6, 9, 158, 169
Australian, 159, 169
authentic, 99
background, 169
caravan, 169
Catholic, 164, 171
challenge, 171, 175
challenges, 157, 160, 165, 166
challenging, 36, 156, 166
charismatic, 163, 164, 165
Christianity, 145, 159, 173, 175
communities, 103
creation, 130
creations, 130
culture, 104
death, 130
divine, 171
educated, 74, 103, 107, 150
emotion, 174
emotionally, 173
equally, 34, 100
faith, 163, 166
family, 169
forgive, 99, 124
free, 99, 124, 130
freeing, 98, 165

God, 12, 13, 31, 32, 33, 34, 36, 97, 98, 100, 108, 129, 130, 145, 146, 147, 148, 154, 155, 156, 157, 158, 159, 160, 161, 163, 164, 165, 166, 167, 169, 170, 171, 173, 174, 175, 176, 177
God's presence, 176
Gold Coast, 6
health, 6
Heaven, 34, 130
history, 104, 156, 167, 170
human, 156, 160
humanity, 99
images, 33, 36, 155, 159
individual, 6
individualistic, 103
inherent, 174
inspiration, 174
inspired, 12, 14, 16, 32, 98, 100, 119, 132, 145, 146, 147, 148, 154, 155, 156, 158, 174
inspired messages, 12, 14, 16, 32, 100, 119, 132, 145, 146, 147, 148, 154, 155, 156, 158, 174
Inspired Messages, 12, 145
institutions, 104
journey, 163
law, 9

life, 9, 74, 107, 148, 150, 156, 160, 163, 166, 174, 176
Life, 31, 36, 37, 198
love, 9, 98, 99, 110, 135, 163, 165, 166, 168
Love, 31, 34, 35, 36
loved, 74, 107, 150
loves, 34, 130, 166
loving, 99
meditation, 155, 159, 161
messages, 16, 32, 74, 107, 145, 146, 147, 148, 151, 154, 161, 174
Mt Warning, 31, 32, 33, 155, 158, 169, 170, 174, 175
natural, 99, 145
one, 74, 104, 107, 150, 170, 175
One God, 16, 31, 148, 174
oneness, 163, 169
person, 165
population, 33
pray, 164, 165, 166
prayer, 155, 159, 161, 165, 174
presence, 170, 171, 174
principal, 164
Prophet, 101
Qur'an, 177
religion, 98
religions, 170
religious, 145, 146, 147, 155, 156, 157, 159, 160, 164, 171

Revelation, 13, 31, 32, 146, 147, 148, 156, 158, 169, 171, 174, 193
Revelations, 12, 31, 32, 33, 100, 145, 146, 148, 154, 155, 158, 161, 171, 174, 175
school, 163, 171
science, 99
Science, 99
scripture, 177
sign, 158, 166, 171, 176, 177
sky, 33
spiritual, 163, 164
spiritually, 173
stories, 16, 31, 32, 148
story, 32, 158
Stradbroke, 33, 158
Straddie, 33, 158
students, 164
sun, 33
teachers, 164, 165
tears, 98, 110, 135, 163, 165, 166, 168, 171, 173, 174, 175
Tears from God, 145, 147, 155, 156, 157, 158, 161, 163, 166, 171, 173, 174, 175, 177, 187
truth, 165
Truth, 170
truthful, 74, 107, 150
twelve, 32, 159
Uluru, 9
USA, 6
western, 98, 167

Word, 169
world, 16, 32, 33, 36, 98,
   103, 130, 145, 147, 148,
   154, 157, 166, 167, 173

world today, 167

Coincidences from GOD???

See Book 4 in *the 'GOD Today' Series,* i.e., *Where's GOD? Revelations Today Photobook Companion: GOD Signs,*

for explanations of unique, exceptional, and challenging photographic examples

of GOD's

signs and coincidences,

which I was extremely fortunate to receive.

It is my favourite book in this *Series*.

BIBLIOGRAPHY

Primary source

GOD – Revelations, Inspired Messages, and Key/Vital Points to the Author from GOD

Secondary Sources

Books and Videos

Ali, Ayaan Hirsi, *Heretic: Why Islam Needs a Reformation Now*, 2015, Harper Collins, New York.

Fishman, R., *No Man's Land*, 2014, Rising Tide Books, Sydney.

Foster, B., *1God.world: One God for All*, 2016, Great Developments Publishers, Gold Coast.

Foster, B., *Where's God? Revelations Today*, 2018, Great Developments Publishers, Gold Coast.

Foster, B., *Where's God? Revelations Today Photobook Companion: GOD'S Signs*, 2018, Great Developments Publishers, Gold Coast.

Foster, B., *Love is the Meaning of Life: GOD'S Love (2nd ed)*, 2020, Great Developments Publishers, Gold Coast.

Foster, B., YouTube videos commenced in 2009 – efozz1 (780+ free videos at this stage)

Wisdom: GOD's Hints & Tips

Tragic Face of Teenage Despair in *The Australian*, 21/3/19, NewsCorp, p.1.

Websites

1God.world in Facebook

Amazon.com: Bryan Foster: Books, Biography, Blog, Audiobooks, Kindle

An Introduction to Discernment – Plenary Council (catholic.org.au)

Bartunek, Fr J., 2015, What is the Gift of Tears'? What exactly is the "Gift of Tears"? -- SpiritualDirection.com

Brahman - Gods or goddesses BBC - Religions - Hinduism: Beliefs

BBC - Religions - Buddhism: Buddhism at a glance

Coronavirus vaccine: Everything you need to know, Coronavirus (COVID-19) vaccine: Options, safety, and how to get it (medicalnewstoday.com)

Crusades, Christianity Crusades | Definition, History, Map, Significance, & Legacy | Britannica

Fenelong, M., (2016) *Receiving the 'gift of tears'* in Our Sunday Visitor, Receiving the 'gift of tears' - Our Sunday Visitor (osvnews.com)

(55) Bryan Foster | LinkedIn

(19) Bryan Foster (@1Godworld1) / Twitter

Foster, B., BRYAN FOSTER AUTHOR

Foster, B., Bryan Foster | God Today | City of Gold Coast (godtodayseries.com)

GCSE BBC, (http://www.bbc.co.uk/schools/gcsebitesize/rs/god/chrevelationrev1.shtml) – page possibly closed?

God Today, Facebook Group (20+) God Today | Facebook

Instagram - Instagram (1godworld)

Islam: Truth or Myth? https://www.bible.ca/islam/islam-history.htm - Bing

Judaism and Numbers Judaism and Numbers | My Jewish Learning

List of religious populations - Wikipedia

Oxford Scholarship Online, Jesus the Fullness of Revelation, Jesus the Fullness of Revelation - Oxford Scholarship (universitypressscholarship.com)

Publisher's new webpage. (Original website started in 2007, closed 12/2018.) BRYAN FOSTER AUTHOR

Rattner, R, The Emotion of Devotion – Crying for God, The Emotion Of Devotion – Crying For God – Silly Sutras

Taylor, F, (2016), Life after death: What did Jesus do between his resurrection and ascension? Life after death: What did Jesus do between his resurrection and ascension? (christiantoday.com)

Tears from God - background - the how, why and when +++ - YouTube video (1) Tears from God - background - the how, why and when +++ - YouTube

The Everyday Prophets are in Our Midst The everyday prophets are in our midst | National Catholic Reporter (ncronline.org)

What is the significance of the number 40 in Judaism? (1) What is the significance of the number 40 in Judaism? - Quora

What is the Significance of Number Forty in Islam? The Significance of the Number 40 in Islam – The Muslim Voice

WISDOM | meaning in the Cambridge English Dictionary dictionary.cambridge.org/dictionary/english/wisdom

All websites viewed in 2020/2021 unless otherwise stated.

Bryan Foster

BOOKS BY AUTHOR

Bryan Foster
& Great Developments Publishers

'GOD Today' Series Books - Out Now

1GOD.world: One GOD for All, (Author Articles) (2016)

Mt Warning GOD's Revelation: Photobook Companion to '1GOD.world', (2017) (available at Apple & Blurb.com only)

Where's GOD? Revelations Today, (Author Articles) (2018)

***Where's GOD? Revelations Today Photobook Companion: GOD Signs (2^{nd}ed) (2018) **(Spectacular, challenging, unique, authentic images from GOD.) **Author's favourite**.

Jesus and Mahomad are GOD (Author Articles) (2020)

Love is the Meaning of Life: GOD'S Love (1^{st}ed) (Author Articles) (2021)

Wisdom: GOD's Hints and Tips (Author Articles) (2021)

Photobooks - Out Now

Mt Warning Wolumbin Circuit: a photographic journey, (2018)

'Straddie' North Stradbroke Island: Photobook of Natural & Shared Beauty, (2019)

12 x photobooks in the *My Australia Photobooks Series* – of Northern Territory, (FNQ) Far North Queensland, (2014-5) and 2 x Mt Warning, NSW (2017-8) by Bryan and Karen Foster

Marketing Books – School and Church - Out Now

School Marketing Manual for the Digital Age (3rd ed), (2008-1st, 2009-2nd, 2011-3rd)

Church Marketing Manual for the Digital Age (2nd ed), (2009-1st, 2011-2nd)

Books Coming

Love is the Meaning of Life (2nd ed) (Author Articles) (appr. 2021/2)

Love is the Meaning of Life GOD'S Love: Photobook Companion (2022)

'*GOD Today* Series* Photographers

Images by

Bryan Foster and Karen Foster
(Geat Developments Publishers)

https://www.bryanfosterauthor.com

https://www.godtodayseries.com

Other Images by

Andrew Foster

(Austographer) in Canada

https://www.Austographer.com

Most photobooks were created from photos taken while on our travels throughout Australia.

'GOD Today' Series (2016-2022)

Written by Author

Bryan Foster.

Published and Copyright

© 2016-2021

by

Great Developments Publishers.

Bryan Foster & Karen Foster - Directors

(Gold Coast, Australia).

Available from good internet bookstores, libraries, and bookstores worldwide.

Bryan Foster

Wisdom: GOD's Hints & Tips

www.ingramcontent.com/pod-product-compliance
Lightning Source LLC
Chambersburg PA
CBHW050311010526
44107CB00055B/2197